# The Overflow of the Heart

For Out of the Overflow of the
Heart the Mouth Speaks

Matthew 12:34

Carolyn Joy

CROSSBOOKS
PUBLISHING

WestBow Press
A Division of Thomas Nelson & Zondervan
1663 Liberty Drive
Bloomington, IN 47403
www.westbowpress.com
1-866-928-1240

ISBN: 978-1-5127-1799-0 (sc)
ISBN: 978-1-5127-0223-1 (hc)
ISBN: 978-1-5127-0224-8 (e)

Dedicated to:

MaKayla Rose
Christian Michael
Selah Sky

My amazing grandchildren who,
with God's grace, have restored my joy.

# Contents

# Introduction

Your *heart* is central to the quality of your life. "For out of the overflow of the *HEART* the mouth speaks" (Matthew 12:34, emphasis added). What was Jesus talking about in Matthew 12:33? He said, "Make a tree good and its fruit will be good, or make a tree bad and its fruit will be bad, for a tree is recognized by its fruit." Likewise, in Matthew 12:35, He said, "The good man brings good things out of the good stored up in him, and the evil man brings evil things out of the evil stored up in him."

Jesus speaks about "the fruit of the Spirit" in Galatians 5:22: "But the fruit of the Spirit is love, joy, peace, patience, kindness, goodness, faithfulness, gentleness and self-control."

The condition of your *heart* is directly related to how you look, speak, and treat others. If your *heart* is whole, you will probably appear happy, speak politely, and treat others with love. If you have a broken *heart*, you will probably appear despondent, speak hurtfully, and treat others callously.

How can you determine the condition of your *heart*? After all, if you want to know the strength of your body, you can take an agility test. If you want to know the condition of your brain, you can take a written test. So how can you tell what is in your *heart* or in the *heart* of someone you meet? The answer is quite simple ... the answer is pressure. The *heart* is a tube, and when pressure is applied, what comes out in words and actions is what is inside.

To understand this principle, think about any and all items you can imagine that come in a tube, such as toothpaste, glue, acrylic paint, hair gel, hair color, cake icing, etc. If these items were all lined up in unmarked tubes, how could you tell what was on the inside? That's easy ... just squeeze the tube. Then you could see, smell, touch, and experience what was inside each tube.

The same is true for a person. When a person is squeezed, you will experience what is inside or what is in the *heart*. It's the substance of the *heart* that will come out. Unlike a tube of icing, we obviously cannot physically squeeze a person. However, you are squeezed every day. Every day, pressure is applied to your daily life. Maybe it is the pressure you feel when you're stuck in traffic and late for work, or maybe it is the pressure you feel when given a deadline on a project. Pressure can be as simple as spilling the milk container on the floor or as difficult as the loss of a loved one. Pressure is love and hate, weddings and divorces. Pressure is a good checkup at the doctor or a diagnosis of cancer. Pressure is going to school, taking tests, making friends, and dealing with enemies. Pressure is around you all the time. How do you react? The substance of your *heart* determines how you react!

Do you react with kindness, patience, forgiveness, and love? Or do you yell, scream, throw something, or hurt someone? If you are honest with yourself, you can gauge your own *heart* and grow to be the person God wants you to become.

Occasionally, you may react in an obscure way—you might overreact to a situation or say something you should have never said. Then, this reaction is usually followed up with an apology and words to the effect of, "I'm sorry ... I didn't really mean what I said." That is a lie. The truth is that you probably did mean what you said, and when pressure was applied, the words that were in your *heart* came out of your mouth! It would be more accurate to say, "I'm sorry I hurt you ... what I was thinking in my head and feeling in my *heart* actually came out of my mouth!"

As Dr. Henry Blackaby states in his devotional *Experiencing God Day by Day*:

> "Jesus said that for every idle word there will be a time of accounting in the day of judgment ... Idle words are things we say carelessly, without concern for their impact on others ... Jesus was fully aware of the devastating nature of our words, for the idle words that come from our mouths give a lucid

picture of the condition of our heart. (Matthew 15:17–20 NKJV) [1]

So from now on, remember the tube scenario. Think about your life in terms of how you react and how you would like to react to external events. The good news is that God can help you change. If you are unhappy with the score on your agility test, you could go to the gym to train and build muscle. If you are unhappy with a written test score, you could hit the books and study more for a better grade. Likewise, if you are not happy with the reaction of your *heart*, you could actively work toward change. Understanding God's desire for your *heart* is the first step to a healthy *heart*.

---

1    Henry T Blackaby & Richard Blackaby, *Experiencing God Day-by-Day,* page 150, (B & H Publishers, 1997), .

# How to Initiate Change

Use the Word of God to transform your life. In order to change your life, you need to change your *heart*. So many times you may seek change, you may pray for change, and yet you may continue along the same path. Whether you seek freedom from addictions, habits, or hang-ups or you seek emotional, physical, and spiritual change, you need to investigate your *heart*.

In Beth Moore's workbook *When Godly People Do Ungodly Things*, she states;

> Much of the body of Christ exists on very little of the actual Word of God. Many of those who get a steady diet of the Word of God don't deliberately receive it (by applying it) through and through. We can get truth into our heads without necessarily letting it get through to the inner recesses of our minds, literally changing the entire way we process thoughts. Likewise, we often let the Word get to our hearts—even bringing us to tears—but don't invite it to take complete residency and authority over our seat of emotions so we can trust some of the things we feel. Further, we say the Word of God is food for our souls, but do we give the Holy Spirit freedom and authority to use it to increasingly transform our entire personalities? [2]

Change can be hard ... it takes commitment. Change can be tough ... it takes dedication. Change can be dangerous ... it takes honesty.

---

2    Beth Moore, *When Godly People Do Ungodly Things*, workbook page 83, (Lifeway Press, 2003), .

When seeking physical change, you can diet or go to the gym and exercise your body. Without commitment to exercise, dedication to the diet, and honesty about what you are eating, you will experience little change. However, with hard work you will see a metamorphosis of your physical *body* right before your eyes.

Addictions and habits can be overwhelming. If you are not honest with yourself and the loved ones around you, there is little hope of overcoming an addiction or habit. But with honesty, commitment, hard work, and God's help, you can transform your *life*.

The same holds true for the *heart*. You need to search your *heart*, hide His Word in your *heart*, and seek Him with all your *heart* (Psalm 139:23; 119:11; Jeremiah 29:13). Then His Word promises, He will give you a new *heart* while giving you the desires of your *heart* (Ezekiel 36:26; Psalm 37:4).

Beth Moore suggests to:

> Start practicing an open dialogue with God concerning your past, present, and future. Talk candidly to Him concerning all weaknesses, temptations, and tendencies to sin. Ask Him on an ongoing basis to reveal any area of your life that you may be unknowingly keeping under lock and key from the reaching, healing power of His word. Approach God as your daily counselor, your soulologist (psyche-ologist) who knows you better than you know yourself. Not only will you find protection, you will discover a level of intimacy with Him unlike anything you've ever experienced. [3]

The Bible is clear that your *heart* affects all aspects of your life.

The wellspring of life comes from your *heart*: "Above all else, guard your *HEART*, for it is the wellspring of life" (Proverbs 4:23, emphasis added).

The *heart* is central to all life, both good and bad: "For the Lord searches every *HEART* and understands every motive behind the thoughts" (1 Chronicles 28:9, emphasis added).

---

3    Beth Moore, *When Godly People Do Ungodly Things,* workbook page 86, (Lifeway Press, 2003), .

2

All emotions and attitude well up in your *heart*: "Man looks at the outward appearance, but the Lord looks at the *HEART*" (1 Samuel 16:7b, emphasis added).

Devotion comes from your *heart*: "Serve the Lord your God with all your *HEART* and all your soul" (Deuteronomy 10:12b, emphasis added).

Reflection comes from your *heart*: "May the words of my mouth and the meditation of my *HEART* be pleasing to your sight, O Lord, my Rock and my Redeemer" (Psalm 19:14, emphasis added).

Purity comes from your *heart*: "Create in me a pure *HEART*, O God, and renew a steadfast spirit within me" (Psalm 51:10, emphasis added).

What you speak comes out of your *heart*: "For out of the overflow of his *HEART* his mouth speaks" (Luke 6:45b, emphasis added).

# How to Use This Devotional

This is not a typical devotional! This is going to take commitment, dedication, and honesty ... plenty of honesty. To change your *heart*, it is going to take serious work. It will not happen overnight. Just like a diet does not create overnight results, so it is with *heart* change ... it needs time. Most people would not be able to give up a habit or addiction in a day. However, with time comes freedom.

God's Word promises to give us a new *heart* if we only seek Him. Ezekiel 36:26 says, "I will give you a new *HEART* and put a new spirit in you; I will remove from you your *HEART* of stone and give you a *HEART* of flesh. And I will put my spirit in you and move you to follow my decrees and be careful to keep my laws" (emphasis added).

You may be experiencing great sorrow and pain or overwhelming joy and blessings. Either way, be honest with God ... He can take it. Let your *heart* flow. Remember, "For out of the overflow of the *HEART* the mouth speaks" (Matthew 12:34, emphasis added) or, in this case, "For out of the overflow of the *heart* the pen writes!" (My personal version.) Let your feelings pour out while your emotions write.

All the Scriptures listed in the back of the book have to do with the *heart*. Read each verse; ponder each thought; scroll through *your* Bible and read the verses before and after each written Scripture. Pick a Scripture that correlates with the way you are feeling or want to feel. The Scriptures in the back of this book are intentionally not grouped by topic so that you will have to read and search the written Scriptures daily for your desired, expressive verse. Write that Scripture at the top of the page. There is no better way to study God's Word than to search Scripture, read it, and then rewrite it. Searching Scripture, reading Scripture, and writing Scripture is exercise equipment for the *heart!* You may copy the Scripture right from the pre-written Scripture pages, or, if you prefer, you can use the Scripture references in the back of the book. Search the Scriptures yourself and then rewrite your chosen verse in the version you like best. If it is a short verse, write the verse more than once. Remember, writing God's Word repeatedly will help you to remember it and embed it into your *heart.*

Then talk to God. Journal your thoughts on that Scripture and how it makes you feel. Write a letter to God. Each letter starts with "Dear God, Today my *heart* overflows with …." Then, continue your devotional journal. There is no right or wrong thought. One day you may tell God, "Today my *heart* overflows with pain and loneliness." The next day you may want to tell God, "Today my *heart* overflows with joy and thanksgiving." Each journal entry will be very specific to what you are feeling and experiencing each time. You may even decide to write the same Scripture for days as you work through your feelings and emotions. Every day your letter to God will be personal.

In traditional devotionals, the Scripture is prewritten at the top of the page, and you have to journal about a topic that someone else has chosen for you. Unlike traditional devotionals, in this devotional, you get to choose the Scripture and the topic you want. You will be able to write your prayer and will never forget what you prayed. You will be able to document answered prayers.

The best part is that you can go back and reread each journal entry to see how you are changing and growing. It is inevitable. God's Word does not return void (Isaiah 55:11). The mere fact that you are forcing yourself to search Scripture on the *heart* will help your *heart* to change and grow.

To help monitor your *heart* change, there is a *heart* ♡ in the beginning of the journal and at the end of each month. Psalm 86:11 says, "Teach me your ways, O Lord, and I will walk in your truth; give me an undivided *HEART,* that I may fear your name" (emphasis added). Do you have a divided *heart?* What is taking up space in your *heart?* Have you given your *heart* wholly to God? Before you begin, take the time to divide up the first *heart* into sections where you are presently spending most of your time. Is God central in your *heart?* Are the fruits of His Spirit evident in your life, or is He a small piece that shares your *heart* with ungodly emotions? After you are finished with each month, there will be another *heart*. Without looking at the first *heart*, divide up the next *heart* according to where your *heart* presently spends the most time. No doubt, you will begin to experience small but steady changes in your *heart*, and with God's help, you will see the fruits of the Spirit grow in your *heart* and life.

The following pages are some examples of how to use this devotional. However, they are just examples. Choose your own Scripture and then write it down. Writing God's Word is great for your soul. Let your own thoughts and emotions overflow with what is inside your *heart*. Write to God, and let Him know how you feel. Let your *heart overflow*!

## Selah

### Pause, Meditate, Listen

# *Date*

*Scripture:* <u>Ephesians 5:19 (NIV): Speak to one another with psalms, hymns, and spiritual songs. Sing and make music in your *heart* to the Lord, always giving thanks to God the</u> <u>Father for everything, in the name of our Lord Jesus Christ.</u>

# *Dear God,*

*Today my heart overflows with* ... <u>praise and thanksgiving. This</u> <u>evening I am closing my thoughts to the past and only focusing on God's</u> <u>goodness and grace. I praise you for your forgiveness. I praise you for your</u> <u>grace and mercy. I praise you for your goodness to me. Thank you, Lord,</u> <u>for adopting me into your family. Thank you, Lord, for taking care of me.</u> <u>Thank you, Lord, for choosing me and setting my path straight. Thank</u> <u>you, Lord, for allowing my heart to cry out in worship. Thank you for</u> <u>focusing my mind on you. Thank you for restoring my soul. I praise you</u> <u>for your goodness and for loving me when I do not deserve your love.</u>

# *Date*

 *Scripture:* John 14:27 (NIV): Peace I leave with you; my peace I give you. I do not give to you as the world gives. Do not let your **hearts** be troubled and do not be afraid.

John 14:27 (NIV): Peace I leave with you; my peace I give you. I do not give to you as the world gives. Do not let your **hearts** be troubled and do not be afraid.

# *Dear God,*

*Today my heart overflows with* ... fear. I am afraid of the future. My **heart** is troubled with the unknown. I need your peace. I need to learn trust. I need to be able to rest in your arms. My mind races with thoughts of past troubles, which leave my soul anxious. My mind races with past mistakes and regrets. I crave peace. I seek peace. I even practice peace. Sometimes I can even experience peace, but most times I am anything but at peace. Most times my heart is hurt, broken, and anxious. Do not let my heart be troubled, and do not let my heart be afraid. Dear God, please calm my anxious **heart,** and grant me your peace.

# Date

♡ *Scripture:* Psalm 51:17 (NIV): The sacrifices of God are a broken spirit; a broken and contrite **heart**, O God, you will not despise.

_____

_____

_____

_____

# Dear God,

*Today my heart overflows with* ... brokenness. As I practice being still and sit in your presence, God, I experience a broken spirit. The loneliness creeps in my heart. The unrest stirs in my soul. I experience moments of comfort and moments of feeling your nearness. I experience mountaintop exposure to you, Lord, and then I roll back down into the valley. Hurt and loneliness feel overwhelming next to promise and hope. Help the mountaintop experiences to exceed the valley moments. Help me to keep my heart and mind stayed and focused on you! Reveal your plan to me, and direct my path so that I may have joy in my heart.

Teach me your way, O Lord, and I will walk in your truth; give me an undivided *HEART*, that I may fear your name.

Psalm 86:11 (emphasis added)

Take the time to divide up the *heart* into sections that indicate where you are presently spending most of your time. Is God central in your *heart*, or is He a small piece? Does your *heart* overflow with love, joy, peace, patience, kindness, goodness, faithfulness, gentleness, and self-control? Does your *heart* overflow with hurt, pain, loneliness, brokenness, anger, and despair? Divide the *heart* so that the sections are proportionate to the majority of emotions you are presently experiencing. There are two examples below.

# *Heart* Monitor #1

Example #1

Example #2

# January 1

♡ Scripture: _____

_____

_____

_____

_____

_____


Dear God,

Today my heart overflows with ... _____

_____

_____

_____

_____

_____

_____

_____

_____

_____

_____

# January 2

♡ *Scripture:* _____

_____

_____

_____

_____

_____


*Dear God,*

*Today my heart overflows with ...* _____

_____

_____

_____

_____

_____

_____

_____

_____

_____

_____

# January 3

♡ Scripture: _____

_____

_____

_____

_____

Dear God,

Today my heart overflows with ... _____

_____

_____

_____

_____

_____

_____

_____

_____

_____

# January 4

♡ Scripture: _____

_____

_____

_____

_____

_____


Dear God,

Today my heart overflows with ... _____

_____

_____

_____

_____

_____

_____

_____

_____

_____

# January 5

♡ Scripture: _____

_____

_____

_____

_____


Dear God,

Today my heart overflows with ... _____

_____

_____

_____

_____

_____

_____

_____

_____

_____

_____

# January 6

♡ Scripture:_____

_____

_____

_____

_____

_____


Dear God,

Today my heart overflows with ... _____

_____

_____

_____

_____

_____

_____

_____

_____

_____

# January 7

♡ Scripture: _____

_____

_____

_____

_____


Dear God,

Today my heart overflows with ... _____

_____

_____

_____

_____

_____

_____

_____

_____

_____

# January 8

♡ Scripture: _____

_____

_____

_____

_____

_____

Dear God,

Today my heart overflows with ... _____

_____

_____

_____

_____

_____

_____

_____

_____

# January 9

♡ Scripture: _____

_____

_____

_____

_____

_____


Dear God,

Today my heart overflows with ... _____

_____

_____

_____

_____

_____

_____

_____

_____

_____

# January 10

♡ Scripture: _____

_____

_____

_____

_____

_____


Dear God,

Today my heart overflows with ... _____

_____

_____

_____

_____

_____

_____

_____

_____

_____

_____

# January 11

♡ Scripture:_____
_____
_____
_____
_____
_____

Dear God,

Today my heart overflows with ... _____
_____
_____
_____
_____
_____
_____
_____
_____
_____
_____

# January 12

♡ Scripture: _____

_____

_____

_____

_____

_____


Dear God,

Today my heart overflows with ... _____

_____

_____

_____

_____

_____

_____

_____

_____

_____

# January 13

♡ Scripture: _____

_____

_____

_____

_____


Dear God,

Today my heart overflows with ... _____

_____

_____

_____

_____

_____

_____

_____

_____

_____

# January 14

♡ Scripture: _____
_____
_____
_____
_____
_____

Dear God,

Today my heart overflows with ... _____
_____
_____
_____
_____
_____
_____
_____
_____
_____
_____
_____

# January 15

♡ *Scripture:* _____

_____

_____

_____

_____

_____


*Dear God,*

*Today my heart overflows with ...* _____

_____

_____

_____

_____

_____

_____

_____

_____

_____

# January 16

♡ Scripture:_____

_____

_____

_____

_____

_____


Dear God,

Today my heart overflows with ... _____

_____

_____

_____

_____

_____

_____

_____

_____

_____

_____

# January 17

♡ Scripture: _____
_____

_____
_____
_____
_____

Dear God,

Today my heart overflows with ... _____
_____
_____
_____
_____
_____
_____
_____
_____
_____
_____
_____

# January 18

♡ Scripture:_____

_____

_____

_____

_____

_____


Dear God,

Today my heart overflows with ... _____

_____

_____

_____

_____

_____

_____

_____

_____

_____

_____

# January 19

♡ Scripture:_____

_____

_____

_____

_____

_____

Dear God,

Today my heart overflows with ..._____

_____

_____

_____

_____

_____

_____

_____

_____

_____

_____

# January 20

♡ Scripture: _____

_____

_____

_____

_____

_____


Dear God,

Today my heart overflows with ... _____

_____

_____

_____

_____

_____

_____

_____

_____

_____

# January 21

♡ Scripture: _____

_____

_____

_____

_____

_____

Dear God,

Today my heart overflows with ... _____

_____

_____

_____

_____

_____

_____

_____

_____

# January 22

♡ Scripture:_____

_____

_____

_____

_____

_____


Dear God,

Today my heart overflows with ... _____

_____

_____

_____

_____

_____

_____

_____

_____

_____

_____

# January 23

♡ Scripture:_____
_____

_____
_____
_____
_____


Dear God,

Today my heart overflows with ... _____
_____
_____
_____
_____
_____
_____
_____
_____
_____
_____
_____

# January 24

♡ Scripture:_____

_____

_____

_____

_____

_____


Dear God,

Today my heart overflows with ... _____

_____

_____

_____

_____

_____

_____

_____

_____

_____

_____

# January 25

♡ Scripture: _____

_____

_____

_____

_____


Dear God,

Today my heart overflows with ... _____

_____

_____

_____

_____

_____

_____

_____

_____

_____

_____

# January 26

♡ Scripture:_____

_____

_____

_____

_____

_____


Dear God,

Today my heart overflows with ... _____

_____

_____

_____

_____

_____

_____

_____

_____

_____

# January 27

♡ Scripture: _____

_____

_____

_____

_____

_____


Dear God,

Today my heart overflows with ... _____

_____

_____

_____

_____

_____

_____

_____

_____

_____

_____

# January 28

♡ Scripture: _____

_____

_____

_____

_____

Dear God,

Today my heart overflows with ... _____

_____

_____

_____

_____

_____

_____

_____

_____

_____

# January 29

♡ Scripture: _____

_____

_____

_____

_____

_____


Dear God,

Today my heart overflows with ... _____

_____

_____

_____

_____

_____

_____

_____

_____

_____

_____

# January 30

♡ Scripture: _____

_____

_____

_____

_____

_____


Dear God,

Today my heart overflows with ... _____

_____

_____

_____

_____

_____

_____

_____

_____

_____

_____

# January 31

♡ Scripture: _____

_____

_____

_____

_____

_____


Dear God,

Today my heart overflows with ... _____

_____

_____

_____

_____

_____

_____

_____

_____

_____

_____

Teach me your way, O Lord, and I will walk in your truth; give me an undivided *HEART*, that I may fear your name.

Psalm 86:11 (emphasis added)

Without looking back at your first divided *Heart*, take the time to divide up this *heart* into sections based on where you're presently spending most of your emotional time. Where does your *heart* spend a majority of its time? Is God central in your *heart*, or is He a small piece? Does your *heart* overflow with love, joy, peace, patience, kindness, goodness, faithfulness, gentleness, and self-control? Does your *heart* overflow with hurt, pain, loneliness, brokenness, anger, and despair? Divide the *heart* so that the sections are proportionate to the majority of emotions you are presently experiencing. After dividing up the *heart* on this page, go back and see how it differs from *Heart* Monitor #1.

# *Heart* Monitor #2

## Selah

### Pause, Meditate, Listen

# February 1

♡ Scripture: _____

_____

_____

_____

_____

_____


Dear God,

Today my heart overflows with ... _____

_____

_____

_____

_____

_____

_____

_____

_____

_____

# February 2

♡ Scripture: _____

_____

_____

_____

_____

_____

Dear God,

Today my heart overflows with ... _____

_____

_____

_____

_____

_____

_____

_____

_____

_____

_____

_____

# February 3

♡ Scripture: _____

_____

_____

_____

_____

_____


Dear God,

Today my heart overflows with ... _____

_____

_____

_____

_____

_____

_____

_____

_____

_____

_____

# February 4

♡ Scripture: _____

_____

_____

_____

_____

Dear God,

Today my heart overflows with ... _____

_____

_____

_____

_____

_____

_____

_____

_____

_____

# February 5

♡ Scripture: _____

_____

_____

_____

_____

_____


Dear God,

Today my heart overflows with ... _____

_____

_____

_____

_____

_____

_____

_____

_____

_____

_____

# February 6

♡ Scripture:_____

_____

_____

_____

_____

_____


Dear God,

Today my heart overflows with ..._____

_____

_____

_____

_____

_____

_____

_____

_____

_____

_____

# February 7

♡ Scripture: _____

_____

_____

_____

_____

_____

Dear God,

Today my heart overflows with ... _____

_____

_____

_____

_____

_____

_____

_____

_____

_____

# February 8

♡ *Scripture:* _____

_____

_____

_____

_____

_____


*Dear God,*

*Today my heart overflows with ...* _____

_____

_____

_____

_____

_____

_____

_____

_____

_____

_____

# February 9

♡ Scripture: _____

_____

_____

_____

_____

_____

Dear God,

Today my heart overflows with ... _____

_____

_____

_____

_____

_____

_____

_____

_____

_____

# February 10

♡ Scripture: _____

_____

_____

_____

_____

_____

Dear God,

Today my heart overflows with ... _____

_____

_____

_____

_____

_____

_____

_____

_____

# February 11

♡ Scripture: _____

_____

_____

_____

_____

_____


Dear God,

Today my heart overflows with ... _____

_____

_____

_____

_____

_____

_____

_____

_____

_____

_____

# February 12

♡ Scripture: _____

_____

_____

_____

_____

_____

Dear God,

Today my heart overflows with ... _____

_____

_____

_____

_____

_____

_____

_____

_____

_____

_____

# February 13

♡ Scripture: _____

_____

_____

_____

_____

Dear God,

Today my heart overflows with ... _____

_____

_____

_____

_____

_____

_____

_____

_____

# February 14

♡ Scripture:_____

_____

_____

_____

_____

_____


Dear God,

Today my heart overflows with ... _____

_____

_____

_____

_____

_____

_____

_____

_____

_____

# February 15

♡ *Scripture:* _____
_____

_____
_____
_____
_____

*Dear God,*

*Today my heart overflows with ...* _____

_____
_____
_____
_____
_____
_____
_____
_____
_____

# February 16

♡ Scripture:_____

_____

_____

_____

_____

_____


Dear God,

Today my heart overflows with ... _____

_____

_____

_____

_____

_____

_____

_____

_____

_____

_____

# February 17

♡ Scripture: _____

_____

_____

_____

_____

_____


Dear God,

Today my heart overflows with ... _____

_____

_____

_____

_____

_____

_____

_____

_____

_____

_____

# February 18

♡ Scripture:_____

_____

_____

_____

_____

_____


Dear God,

Today my heart overflows with ... _____

_____

_____

_____

_____

_____

_____

_____

_____

_____

_____

# February 19

♡ Scripture: _____

_____

_____

_____

_____

_____

Dear God,

Today my heart overflows with ... _____

_____

_____

_____

_____

_____

_____

_____

_____

_____

# February 20

♡ Scripture:_____

_____

_____

_____

_____

_____

Dear God,

Today my heart overflows with ... _____

_____

_____

_____

_____

_____

_____

_____

_____

_____

_____

# February 21

♡ Scripture:_____
_____
_____
_____
_____
_____


Dear God,

Today my heart overflows with ... _____
_____
_____
_____
_____
_____
_____
_____
_____
_____
_____
_____

# February 22

♡ Scripture:_____

_____

_____

_____

_____

_____



Dear God,

Today my heart overflows with ... _____

_____

_____

_____

_____

_____

_____

_____

_____

_____

# February 23

♡ Scripture: _____

_____

_____

_____

_____

_____


Dear God,

Today my heart overflows with ... _____

_____

_____

_____

_____

_____

_____

_____

_____

_____

_____

# February 24

♡ Scripture: _____

_____

_____

_____

_____

_____


Dear God,

Today my heart overflows with ... _____

_____

_____

_____

_____

_____

_____

_____

_____

_____

# February 25

♡ Scripture: _____

_____

_____

_____

_____

Dear God,

Today my heart overflows with ... _____

_____

_____

_____

_____

_____

_____

_____

_____

_____

# February 26

♡ Scripture:_____

_____

_____

_____

_____

_____


Dear God,

Today my heart overflows with ... _____

_____

_____

_____

_____

_____

_____

_____

_____

_____

# February 27

♡ Scripture: _____

_____

_____

_____

_____

_____

Dear God,

Today my heart overflows with ... _____

_____

_____

_____

_____

_____

_____

_____

_____

_____

# February 28

♡ Scripture: _____

_____

_____

_____

_____

_____


Dear God,

Today my heart overflows with ... _____

_____

_____

_____

_____

_____

_____

_____

_____

_____

# February 29

♡ Scripture: _____

_____

_____

_____

_____

_____


Dear God,

Today my heart overflows with ... _____

_____

_____

_____

_____

_____

_____

_____

_____

Teach me your way, O Lord, and I will walk in your truth; give me an undivided *HEART*, that I may fear your name.
Psalm 86:11 (emphasis added)

Without looking back at your last divided *heart*, take the time to divide up this *heart* into sections based on where you're presently spending most of your emotional time. Where does your *heart* spend a majority of its time? Is God central in your *heart*, or is He a small piece? Does your *heart* overflow with love, joy, peace, patience, kindness, goodness, faithfulness, gentleness, and self-control? Does your *heart* overflow with hurt, pain, loneliness, brokenness, anger, and despair? Divide the *heart* so that the sections are proportionate to the majority of emotions you are presently experiencing. After dividing up the *heart* on this page, go back and see how it differs from Heart Monitor *#1 and #2*.

# *Heart* Monitor #3

## *Selah*
### *Pause, Meditate, Listen*

# March 1

♡ Scripture: _____

_____

_____

_____

_____

_____

Dear God,

Today my heart overflows with ... _____

_____

_____

_____

_____

_____

_____

_____

_____

_____

# March 2

♡ Scripture:_____
_____
_____
_____
_____
_____

Dear God,

Today my heart overflows with ... _____
_____
_____
_____
_____
_____
_____
_____
_____
_____

# March 3

♡ *Scripture:* _____
_____
_____
_____
_____
_____

*Dear God,*

*Today my heart overflows with ...* _____
_____
_____
_____
_____
_____
_____
_____
_____
_____
_____

# March 4

♡ *Scripture:* _____
_____
_____
_____
_____
_____

*Dear God,*

*Today my heart overflows with ...* _____
_____
_____
_____
_____
_____
_____
_____
_____
_____
_____

# March 5

♡ Scripture: _____

_____

_____

_____

_____

_____


Dear God,

Today my heart overflows with ... _____

_____

_____

_____

_____

_____

_____

_____

_____

_____

_____

# March 6

♡ Scripture:_____

_____

_____

_____

_____

_____


Dear God,

Today my heart overflows with ... _____

_____

_____

_____

_____

_____

_____

_____

_____

_____

_____

# March 7

♡ Scripture: _____

_____

_____

_____

_____


Dear God,

Today my heart overflows with ... _____

_____

_____

_____

_____

_____

_____

_____

_____

# March 8

♡ Scripture:_____

_____

_____

_____

_____

_____


Dear God,

Today my heart overflows with ... _____

_____

_____

_____

_____

_____

_____

_____

_____

_____

_____

# March 9

♡ *Scripture:* _____

_____

_____

_____

_____

_____


*Dear God,*

*Today my heart overflows with ...* _____

_____

_____

_____

_____

_____

_____

_____

_____

_____

_____

# March 10

♡ Scripture:_____

_____

_____

_____

_____

_____



Dear God,

Today my heart overflows with ... _____

_____

_____

_____

_____

_____

_____

_____

_____

_____

# March 11

♡ Scripture: _____
_____
_____
_____
_____
_____

Dear God,

Today my heart overflows with ... _____
_____
_____
_____
_____
_____
_____
_____
_____
_____
_____

# March 12

♡ Scripture:_____

_____

_____

_____

_____

_____


Dear God,

Today my heart overflows with ... _____

_____

_____

_____

_____

_____

_____

_____

_____

_____

_____

_____

# March 13

♡ Scripture: _____

_____

_____

_____

_____

_____


Dear God,

Today my heart overflows with ... _____

_____

_____

_____

_____

_____

_____

_____

_____

_____

_____

# March 14

♡ Scripture:_____
_____
_____
_____
_____
_____

Dear God,

Today my heart overflows with ... _____
_____
_____
_____
_____
_____
_____
_____
_____
_____
_____

# March 15

♡ Scripture:_____

_____

_____

_____

_____

_____


Dear God,

Today my heart overflows with ... _____

_____

_____

_____

_____

_____

_____

_____

_____

_____

_____

# March 16

♡ Scripture: _____

_____

_____

_____

_____

_____

Dear God,

Today my heart overflows with ... _____

_____

_____

_____

_____

_____

_____

_____

_____

_____

_____

# March 17

♡ Scripture: _____

_____

_____

_____

_____


Dear God,

Today my heart overflows with ... _____

_____

_____

_____

_____

_____

_____

_____

_____

_____

# March 18

♡ Scripture:_____

_____

_____

_____

_____

Dear God,

Today my heart overflows with ... _____

_____

_____

_____

_____

_____

_____

_____

_____

_____

# March 19

♡ Scripture:_____

_____

_____

_____

_____

_____


Dear God,

Today my heart overflows with ... _____

_____

_____

_____

_____

_____

_____

_____

_____

_____

# March 20

♡ Scripture:_____

_____

_____

_____

_____

_____


Dear God,

Today my heart overflows with ... _____

_____

_____

_____

_____

_____

_____

_____

_____

_____

# March 21

♡ Scripture:_____
_____
_____
_____
_____
_____

Dear God,

Today my heart overflows with ... _____
_____
_____
_____
_____
_____
_____
_____
_____
_____
_____

# March 22

♡ Scripture: _____
_____
_____
_____
_____
_____

Dear God,

Today my heart overflows with ... _____
_____
_____
_____
_____
_____
_____
_____
_____
_____

# March 23

♡ Scripture: _____
_____
_____
_____
_____
_____

Dear God,

Today my heart overflows with ... _____
_____
_____
_____
_____
_____
_____
_____
_____
_____
_____

# March 24

♡ Scripture: _____

_____

_____

_____

_____


Dear God,

Today my heart overflows with ... _____

_____

_____

_____

_____

_____

_____

_____

_____

_____

_____

# March 25

♡ *Scripture:* _____
_____
_____
_____
_____
_____

*Dear God,*

*Today my heart overflows with ...* _____
_____
_____
_____
_____
_____
_____
_____
_____
_____
_____

# March 26

♡ Scripture: _____

_____

_____

_____

_____

_____


Dear God,

Today my heart overflows with ... _____

_____

_____

_____

_____

_____

_____

_____

_____

_____

# March 27

♡ Scripture: _____
_____
_____
_____
_____
_____

Dear God,

Today my heart overflows with ... _____
_____
_____
_____
_____
_____
_____
_____
_____
_____
_____

# March 28

♡ *Scripture:* _____

_____

_____

_____

_____

_____


*Dear God,*

*Today my heart overflows with ...* _____

_____

_____

_____

_____

_____

_____

_____

_____

_____

# March 29

♡ Scripture: _____

_____

_____

_____

_____

_____

Dear God,

Today my heart overflows with ... _____

_____

_____

_____

_____

_____

_____

_____

_____

_____

# March 30

♡ Scripture: _____

_____

_____

_____

_____

_____


Dear God,

Today my heart overflows with ... _____

_____

_____

_____

_____

_____

_____

_____

_____

_____

# March 31

♡ Scripture: _____

_____

_____

_____

_____


Dear God,

Today my heart overflows with ... _____

_____

_____

_____

_____

_____

_____

_____

_____

_____

_____

Teach me your way, O Lord, and I will walk in your truth; give me an undivided *HEART*, that I may fear your name.
Psalm 86:11 (emphasis added)

Without looking back at your previous divided *heart*, take the time to divide up this *heart* into sections based on where you're presently spending most of your emotional time. Where does your *heart* spend a majority of its time? Is God central in your *heart*, or is He a small piece? Does your *heart* overflow with love, joy, peace, patience, kindness, goodness, faithfulness, gentleness, and self-control? Does your *heart* overflow with hurt, pain, loneliness, brokenness, anger, and despair? Divide the *heart* so that the sections are proportionate to the majority of emotions you are presently experiencing. After dividing up the *heart* on this page, go back and see how it differs from previous *hearts*.

# *Heart* Monitor #4

## *Selah*

### *Pause, Meditate, Listen*

# April 1

♡ Scripture: _____

_____

_____

_____

_____

_____


Dear God,

Today my heart overflows with ... _____

_____

_____

_____

_____

_____

_____

_____

_____

_____

# April 2

♡ Scripture:_____

_____

_____

_____

_____

_____


Dear God,

Today my heart overflows with ... _____

_____

_____

_____

_____

_____

_____

_____

_____

_____

# April 3

♡ Scripture: _____

_____

_____

_____

_____

_____


Dear God,

Today my heart overflows with ... _____

_____

_____

_____

_____

_____

_____

_____

_____

_____

_____

# April 4

♡ Scripture:_____

_____

_____

_____

_____

_____


Dear God,

Today my heart overflows with ... _____

_____

_____

_____

_____

_____

_____

_____

_____

# April 5

♡ Scripture: _____

_____

_____

_____

_____

_____


Dear God,

Today my heart overflows with ... _____

_____

_____

_____

_____

_____

_____

_____

_____

_____

_____

# April 6

♡ Scripture: _____

_____

_____

_____

_____

_____


Dear God,

Today my heart overflows with ... _____

_____

_____

_____

_____

_____

_____

_____

_____

_____

# April 7

♡ Scripture: _____

_____

_____

_____

_____

_____


Dear God,

Today my heart overflows with ... _____

_____

_____

_____

_____

_____

_____

_____

_____

_____

_____

# April 8

♡ Scripture: _____

_____

_____

_____

_____

_____


Dear God,

Today my heart overflows with ... _____

_____

_____

_____

_____

_____

_____

_____

_____

_____

# April 9

♡ Scripture: _____

_____

_____

_____

_____

Dear God,

Today my heart overflows with ... _____

_____

_____

_____

_____

_____

_____

_____

_____

# April 10

♡ Scripture: _____
_____
_____
_____
_____
_____

Dear God,

Today my heart overflows with ... _____
_____
_____
_____
_____
_____
_____
_____
_____
_____
_____

# April 11

♡ Scripture: _____

_____

_____

_____

_____

_____


Dear God,

Today my heart overflows with ... _____

_____

_____

_____

_____

_____

_____

_____

_____

_____

# April 12

♡ Scripture: _____

_____

_____

_____

_____

_____


Dear God,

Today my heart overflows with ... _____

_____

_____

_____

_____

_____

_____

_____

_____

_____

# April 13

♡ Scripture: _____

_____

_____

_____

_____

_____


Dear God,

Today my heart overflows with ... _____

_____

_____

_____

_____

_____

_____

_____

_____

_____

_____

# April 14

♡ Scripture:_____
_____

_____
_____
_____
_____

Dear God,

Today my heart overflows with ... _____
_____
_____
_____
_____
_____
_____
_____
_____
_____
_____

# April 15

♡ Scripture: _____

_____

_____

_____

_____

_____


Dear God,

Today my heart overflows with ... _____

_____

_____

_____

_____

_____

_____

_____

_____

_____

_____

# April 16

♡ Scripture:_____

_____

_____

_____

_____

_____

Dear God,

Today my heart overflows with ... _____

_____

_____

_____

_____

_____

_____

_____

_____

_____

# April 17

♡ *Scripture:* _____

_____

_____

_____

_____

_____

*Dear God,*

*Today my heart overflows with ...* _____

_____

_____

_____

_____

_____

_____

_____

_____

_____

# April 18

♡ Scripture:_____
_____
_____
_____
_____
_____

Dear God,

Today my heart overflows with ... _____
_____
_____
_____
_____
_____
_____
_____
_____
_____
_____

# April 19

♡ Scripture:_____

_____

_____

_____

_____

_____


Dear God,

Today my heart overflows with ... _____

_____

_____

_____

_____

_____

_____

_____

_____

_____

_____

# April 20

♡ Scripture:_____

_____

_____

_____

_____

_____


Dear God,

Today my heart overflows with ... _____

_____

_____

_____

_____

_____

_____

_____

_____

_____

# April 21

♡ Scripture:_____

_____

_____

_____

_____

_____


Dear God,

Today my heart overflows with ... _____

_____

_____

_____

_____

_____

_____

_____

_____

_____

_____

# April 22

♡ Scripture: _____

_____

_____

_____

_____

_____


Dear God,

Today my heart overflows with ... _____

_____

_____

_____

_____

_____

_____

_____

_____

_____

_____

# April 23

♡ Scripture: _____

_____

_____

_____

_____

_____


Dear God,

Today my heart overflows with ... _____

_____

_____

_____

_____

_____

_____

_____

_____

_____

# April 24

♡ Scripture: _____

_____

_____

_____

_____

_____


Dear God,

Today my heart overflows with ... _____

_____

_____

_____

_____

_____

_____

_____

_____

_____

# April 25

♡ Scripture:_____

_____

_____

_____

_____

_____


Dear God,

Today my heart overflows with ... _____

_____

_____

_____

_____

_____

_____

_____

_____

_____

# April 26

♡ Scripture: _____

_____

_____

_____

_____

_____


Dear God,

Today my heart overflows with ... _____

_____

_____

_____

_____

_____

_____

_____

_____

_____

# April 27

♡ Scripture:_____

_____

_____

_____

_____

_____

Dear God,

Today my heart overflows with ... _____

_____

_____

_____

_____

_____

_____

_____

_____

_____

# April 28

♡ Scripture: _____

_____

_____

_____

_____

_____


Dear God,

Today my heart overflows with ... _____

_____

_____

_____

_____

_____

_____

_____

_____

_____

_____

# April 29

♡ Scripture: _____

_____

_____

_____

_____

_____


Dear God,

Today my heart overflows with ... _____

_____

_____

_____

_____

_____

_____

_____

_____

_____

_____

# April 30

♡ Scripture: _____

_____

_____

_____

_____

_____


Dear God,

Today my heart overflows with ... _____

_____

_____

_____

_____

_____

_____

_____

_____

_____

_____

Teach me your way, O Lord, and I will walk in your truth;
give me an undivided *HEART*, that I may fear your name.
Psalm 86:11 (emphasis added)

Without looking back at your previous divided *heart*, take the time to divide up this *heart* into sections based on where you're presently spending most of your emotional time. Where does your *heart* spend a majority of its time? Is God central in your *heart,* or is He a small piece? Does your *heart* overflow with love, joy, peace, patience, kindness, goodness, faithfulness, gentleness, and self-control? Does your *heart* overflow with hurt, pain, loneliness, brokenness, anger, and despair? Divide the *heart* so that the sections are proportionate to the majority of emotions you are presently experiencing. After dividing up the *heart* on this page, go back and see how it differs from previous *hearts.* Can you see your *heart* changing?

# *Heart* Monitor #5

## *Selah*

### *Pause, Meditate, Listen*

# May 1

♡ Scripture: _____

_____

_____

_____

_____

_____


Dear God,

Today my heart overflows with ... _____

_____

_____

_____

_____

_____

_____

_____

_____

_____

# May 2

♡ Scripture: _____

_____

_____

_____

_____

Dear God,

Today my heart overflows with ... _____

_____

_____

_____

_____

_____

_____

_____

_____

# May 3

♡ Scripture: _____

_____

_____

_____

_____

_____


Dear God,

Today my heart overflows with ... _____

_____

_____

_____

_____

_____

_____

_____

_____

_____

# May 4

♡ Scripture: _____

_____

_____

_____

_____

_____


Dear God,

Today my heart overflows with ... _____

_____

_____

_____

_____

_____

_____

_____

_____

_____

_____

# May 5

♡ Scripture:_____
_____

_____
_____
_____
_____

Dear God,

Today my heart overflows with ... _____

_____
_____
_____
_____
_____
_____
_____
_____
_____
_____

# May 6

♡ Scripture: _____

_____

_____

_____

_____

_____


Dear God,

Today my heart overflows with ... _____

_____

_____

_____

_____

_____

_____

_____

_____

_____

# May 7

♡ Scripture:_____

_____

_____

_____

_____

_____


Dear God,

Today my heart overflows with ... _____

_____

_____

_____

_____

_____

_____

_____

_____

_____

_____

_____

# May 8

♡ Scripture: _____

_____

_____

_____

_____

_____


Dear God,

Today my heart overflows with ... _____

_____

_____

_____

_____

_____

_____

_____

_____

_____

# May 9

♡ Scripture: _____

_____

_____

_____

_____

_____


Dear God,

Today my heart overflows with ... _____

_____

_____

_____

_____

_____

_____

_____

_____

_____

# May 10

♡ Scripture: _____

_____

_____

_____

_____

_____


Dear God,

Today my heart overflows with ... _____

_____

_____

_____

_____

_____

_____

_____

_____

_____

_____

# May 11

♡ Scripture:_____

_____

_____

_____

_____

_____


Dear God,

Today my heart overflows with ... _____

_____

_____

_____

_____

_____

_____

_____

_____

_____

# May 12

♡ Scripture: _____

_____

_____

_____

_____

_____

Dear God,

Today my heart overflows with ... _____

_____

_____

_____

_____

_____

_____

_____

_____

_____

# May 13

♡ Scripture:_____
_____
_____
_____
_____
_____

Dear God,

Today my heart overflows with ... _____
_____
_____
_____
_____
_____
_____
_____
_____
_____
_____

# May 14

♡ Scripture:_____

_____

_____

_____

_____

_____

Dear God,

Today my heart overflows with ... _____

_____

_____

_____

_____

_____

_____

_____

_____

_____

# May 15

♡ Scripture:_____

_____

_____

_____

_____

_____



Dear God,

Today my heart overflows with ... _____

_____

_____

_____

_____

_____

_____

_____

_____

_____

# May 16

♡ Scripture: _____

_____

_____

_____

_____

_____


Dear God,

Today my heart overflows with ... _____

_____

_____

_____

_____

_____

_____

_____

_____

_____

_____

# May 17

♡ Scripture:_____
_____
_____
_____
_____
_____


Dear God,

Today my heart overflows with ... _____
_____
_____
_____
_____
_____
_____
_____
_____
_____

# May 18

♡ Scripture:_____
_____

_____
_____
_____
_____


Dear God,

Today my heart overflows with ... _____

_____
_____
_____
_____
_____
_____
_____
_____
_____
_____

# May 19

♡ Scripture: _____

_____

_____

_____

_____

_____


Dear God,

Today my heart overflows with ... _____

_____

_____

_____

_____

_____

_____

_____

_____

_____

_____

# May 20

♡ Scripture: _____

_____

_____

_____

_____

_____

Dear God,

Today my heart overflows with ... _____

_____

_____

_____

_____

_____

_____

_____

_____

_____

# May 21

♡ Scripture: _____

_____

_____

_____

_____

_____


Dear God,

Today my heart overflows with ... _____

_____

_____

_____

_____

_____

_____

_____

_____

_____

_____

# May 22

♡ Scripture:_____

_____

_____

_____

_____

_____

Dear God,

Today my heart overflows with ... _____

_____

_____

_____

_____

_____

_____

_____

_____

_____

# May 23

♡ Scripture:_____

_____

_____

_____

_____

_____

Dear God,

Today my heart overflows with ... _____

_____

_____

_____

_____

_____

_____

_____

_____

_____

# May 24

♡ Scripture: _____
_____
_____
_____
_____
_____

Dear God,

Today my heart overflows with ... _____
_____
_____
_____
_____
_____
_____
_____
_____
_____
_____

# May 25

♡ Scripture:_____

_____

_____

_____

_____

_____


Dear God,

Today my heart overflows with ... _____

_____

_____

_____

_____

_____

_____

_____

_____

_____

_____

# May 26

♡ *Scripture:* _____

_____

_____

_____

_____

_____

*Dear God,*

*Today my heart overflows with ...* _____

_____

_____

_____

_____

_____

_____

_____

_____

_____

_____

# May 27

♡ Scripture: _____

_____

_____

_____

_____

Dear God,

Today my heart overflows with ... _____

_____

_____

_____

_____

_____

_____

_____

_____

_____

# May 28

♡ Scripture:_____

_____

_____

_____

_____

_____


Dear God,

Today my heart overflows with ... _____

_____

_____

_____

_____

_____

_____

_____

_____

_____

# May 29

♡ Scripture:_____

_____

_____

_____

_____

_____


Dear God,

Today my heart overflows with ... _____

_____

_____

_____

_____

_____

_____

_____

_____

_____

# May 30

♡ Scripture: _____

_____

_____

_____

_____

_____

Dear God,

Today my heart overflows with ... _____

_____

_____

_____

_____

_____

_____

_____

_____

_____

# May 31

♡ Scripture: _____

_____

_____

_____

_____

_____


Dear God,

Today my heart overflows with ... _____

_____

_____

_____

_____

_____

_____

_____

_____

_____

Teach me your way, O Lord, and I will walk in your truth; give me an undivided *HEART*, that I may fear your name. Psalm 86:11 (emphasis added)

Without looking back at your previous divided *heart*, take the time to divide up this *heart* into sections based on where you're presently spending most of your emotional time. Where does your *heart* spend a majority of its time? Is God central in your *heart*, or is He a small piece? Does your *heart* overflow with love, joy, peace, patience, kindness, goodness, faithfulness, gentleness, and self-control? Does your *heart* overflow with hurt, pain, loneliness, brokenness, anger, and despair? Divide the *heart* so that the sections are proportionate to the majority of emotions you are presently experiencing. After dividing up the *heart* on this page, go back and see how it differs from previous *hearts*. Are you experiencing a changed *heart*?

# *Heart* Monitor #6

## *Selah*

### *Pause, Meditate, Listen*

# June 1

♡ Scripture: _____

_____

_____

_____

_____


Dear God,

Today my heart overflows with ... _____

_____

_____

_____

_____

_____

_____

_____

_____

_____

# June 2

♡ Scripture:_____

_____

_____

_____

_____

_____

Dear God,

Today my heart overflows with ... _____

_____

_____

_____

_____

_____

_____

_____

_____

_____

# June 3

♡ Scripture: _____

_____

_____

_____

_____

_____

Dear God,

Today my heart overflows with ... _____

_____

_____

_____

_____

_____

_____

_____

_____

_____

# June 4

♡ Scripture:_____
_____
_____
_____
_____
_____

Dear God,

Today my heart overflows with ... _____
_____
_____
_____
_____
_____
_____
_____
_____
_____

# June 5

♡ Scripture: _____
_____
_____
_____
_____
_____

Dear God,

Today my heart overflows with ... _____
_____
_____
_____
_____
_____
_____
_____
_____
_____
_____

# June 6

♡ Scripture: _____

_____

_____

_____

_____

_____


Dear God,

Today my heart overflows with ... _____

_____

_____

_____

_____

_____

_____

_____

_____

_____

# June 7

♡ Scripture: _____
_____

_____

_____

_____

_____

Dear God,

Today my heart overflows with ... _____

_____

_____

_____

_____

_____

_____

_____

_____

_____

_____

# June 8

♡ *Scripture:*_____

_____

_____

_____

_____

_____


*Dear God,*

*Today my heart overflows with ...* _____

_____

_____

_____

_____

_____

_____

_____

_____

_____

_____

# June 9

♡ Scripture:_____
_____

_____
_____
_____
_____

Dear God,

Today my heart overflows with ... _____

_____
_____
_____
_____
_____
_____
_____
_____
_____
_____

# June 10

♡ Scripture:_____

_____

_____

_____

_____

_____

Dear God,

Today my heart overflows with ... _____

_____

_____

_____

_____

_____

_____

_____

_____

_____

_____

# June 11

♡ Scripture: _____
_____

_____
_____
_____
_____

Dear God,

Today my heart overflows with ... _____

_____
_____
_____
_____
_____
_____
_____
_____
_____
_____

# June 12

♡ Scripture: _____

_____

_____

_____

_____

_____


Dear God,

Today my heart overflows with ... _____

_____

_____

_____

_____

_____

_____

_____

_____

_____

# June 13

♡ Scripture: _____

_____

_____

_____

_____

_____


Dear God,

Today my heart overflows with ... _____

_____

_____

_____

_____

_____

_____

_____

_____

_____

_____

# June 14

♡ Scripture:_____

_____

_____

_____

_____

_____


Dear God,

Today my heart overflows with ... _____

_____

_____

_____

_____

_____

_____

_____

_____

_____

_____

# June 15

♡ Scripture: _____

_____

_____

_____

_____

_____


Dear God,

Today my heart overflows with ... _____

_____

_____

_____

_____

_____

_____

_____

_____

_____

_____

_____

# June 16

♡ Scripture: _____

_____

_____

_____

_____

_____


Dear God,

Today my heart overflows with ... _____

_____

_____

_____

_____

_____

_____

_____

_____

_____

_____

_____

# June 17

♡ Scripture:_____
_____

_____
_____
_____
_____

Dear God,

Today my heart overflows with ... _____

_____
_____
_____
_____
_____
_____
_____
_____
_____
_____

# June 18

♡ Scripture: _____

_____

_____

_____

_____

_____


Dear God,

Today my heart overflows with ... _____

_____

_____

_____

_____

_____

_____

_____

_____

_____

# June 19

♡ Scripture: _____

_____

_____

_____

_____

_____


Dear God,

Today my heart overflows with ... _____

_____

_____

_____

_____

_____

_____

_____

_____

_____

_____

# June 20

♡ Scripture:_____

_____

_____

_____

_____

_____

Dear God,

Today my heart overflows with ... _____

_____

_____

_____

_____

_____

_____

_____

_____

_____

# June 21

♡ Scripture:_____

_____

_____

_____

_____

_____


Dear God,

Today my heart overflows with ..._____

_____

_____

_____

_____

_____

_____

_____

_____

_____

_____

# June 22

♡ Scripture:_____

_____

_____

_____

_____

_____


Dear God,

Today my heart overflows with ... _____

_____

_____

_____

_____

_____

_____

_____

_____

_____

_____

# June 23

♡ Scripture: _____
_____
_____
_____
_____
_____

Dear God,

Today my heart overflows with ... _____
_____
_____
_____
_____
_____
_____
_____
_____
_____
_____
_____

# June 24

♡ Scripture: _____

_____

_____

_____

_____

_____


Dear God,

Today my heart overflows with ... _____

_____

_____

_____

_____

_____

_____

_____

_____

_____

# June 25

♡ Scripture: _____

_____

_____

_____

_____

_____


Dear God,

Today my heart overflows with ... _____

_____

_____

_____

_____

_____

_____

_____

_____

_____

# June 26

♡ Scripture:_____

_____

_____

_____

_____

_____

Dear God,

Today my heart overflows with ... _____

_____

_____

_____

_____

_____

_____

_____

_____

_____

# June 27

♡ Scripture: _____

_____

_____

_____

_____

_____


Dear God,

Today my heart overflows with ... _____

_____

_____

_____

_____

_____

_____

_____

_____

_____

_____

# June 28

♡ Scripture: _____
_____

_____
_____
_____
_____

Dear God,

Today my heart overflows with ... _____

_____
_____
_____
_____
_____
_____
_____
_____
_____

# June 29

♡ Scripture: _____

_____

_____

_____

_____

_____


Dear God,

Today my heart overflows with ... _____

_____

_____

_____

_____

_____

_____

_____

_____

_____

_____

# June 30

♡ Scripture: _____

_____

_____

_____

_____

_____


Dear God,

Today my heart overflows with ... _____

_____

_____

_____

_____

_____

_____

_____

_____

_____

_____

Teach me your way, O Lord, and I will walk in your truth; give me an undivided *HEART*, that I may fear your name.

Psalm 86:11 (emphasis added)

Without looking back at your previous divided *heart*, take the time to divide up this *heart* into sections based on where you're presently spending most of your emotional time. Where does your *heart* spend a majority of its time? Is God central in your *heart*, or is He a small piece? Does your *heart* overflow with love, joy, peace, patience, kindness, goodness, faithfulness, gentleness, and self-control? Does your *heart* overflow with hurt, pain, loneliness, brokenness, anger, and despair? Divide the *heart* so that the sections are proportionate to the majority of emotions you are presently experiencing. After dividing up the *heart* on this page, go back and see how it differs from previous *hearts*. Are you experiencing a changed *heart*?

# *Heart* Monitor #7

## *Selah*

*Pause, Meditate, Listen*

# July 1

♡ Scripture: _____
_____
_____
_____
_____
_____

Dear God,

Today my heart overflows with ... _____
_____
_____
_____
_____
_____
_____
_____
_____
_____
_____

# July 2

♡ Scripture: _____

_____

_____

_____

_____

_____


Dear God,

Today my heart overflows with ... _____

_____

_____

_____

_____

_____

_____

_____

_____

_____

_____

# July 3

♡ Scripture: _____
_____
_____
_____
_____
_____

Dear God,

Today my heart overflows with ... _____
_____
_____
_____
_____
_____
_____
_____
_____
_____
_____

# July 4

♡ Scripture: _____

_____

_____

_____

_____

_____


Dear God,

Today my heart overflows with ... _____

_____

_____

_____

_____

_____

_____

_____

_____

_____

_____

# July 5

♡ Scripture: _____

_____

_____

_____

_____

_____

Dear God,

Today my heart overflows with ... _____

_____

_____

_____

_____

_____

_____

_____

_____

_____

# July 6

♡ Scripture: _____

_____

_____

_____

_____

_____


Dear God,

Today my heart overflows with ... _____

_____

_____

_____

_____

_____

_____

_____

_____

_____

# July 7

♡ Scripture: _____
_____
_____
_____
_____
_____

Dear God,

Today my heart overflows with ... _____
_____
_____
_____
_____
_____
_____
_____
_____
_____
_____
_____

# July 8

♡ Scripture: _____

_____

_____

_____

_____

_____

Dear God,

Today my heart overflows with ... _____

_____

_____

_____

_____

_____

_____

_____

_____

_____

# July 9

♡ Scripture: _____

_____

_____

_____

_____

_____


Dear God,

Today my heart overflows with ... _____

_____

_____

_____

_____

_____

_____

_____

_____

_____

# July 10

♡ Scripture:_____

_____

_____

_____

_____

_____


Dear God,

Today my heart overflows with ... _____

_____

_____

_____

_____

_____

_____

_____

_____

_____

_____

# July 11

♡ Scripture: _____

_____

_____

_____

_____

_____


Dear God,

Today my heart overflows with ... _____

_____

_____

_____

_____

_____

_____

_____

_____

_____

_____

# July 12

♡ Scripture:_____

_____

_____

_____

_____

_____


Dear God,

Today my heart overflows with ... _____

_____

_____

_____

_____

_____

_____

_____

_____

_____

_____

# July 13

♡ Scripture:_____

_____

_____

_____

_____

_____


Dear God,

Today my heart overflows with ... _____

_____

_____

_____

_____

_____

_____

_____

_____

# July 14

♡ *Scripture:* _____

_____

_____

_____

_____

_____

*Dear God,*

*Today my heart overflows with ...* _____

_____

_____

_____

_____

_____

_____

_____

_____

_____

# July 15

♡ Scripture: _____

_____

_____

_____

_____

_____


Dear God,

Today my heart overflows with ... _____

_____

_____

_____

_____

_____

_____

_____

_____

_____

_____

# July 16

♡ Scripture: _____

_____

_____

_____

_____

_____

Dear God,

Today my heart overflows with ... _____

_____

_____

_____

_____

_____

_____

_____

_____

_____

_____

# July 17

♡ Scripture: _____

_____

_____

_____

_____

_____


Dear God,

Today my heart overflows with ... _____

_____

_____

_____

_____

_____

_____

_____

_____

_____

_____

# July 18

♡ Scripture:_____

_____

_____

_____

_____

_____


Dear God,

Today my heart overflows with ... _____

_____

_____

_____

_____

_____

_____

_____

_____

_____

# July 19

♡ Scripture: _____
_____
_____
_____
_____
_____

Dear God,

Today my heart overflows with ... _____
_____
_____
_____
_____
_____
_____
_____
_____
_____
_____

# July 20

♡ Scripture: _____

_____

_____

_____

_____

_____


Dear God,

Today my heart overflows with ... _____

_____

_____

_____

_____

_____

_____

_____

_____

_____

_____

# July 21

♡ Scripture: _____

_____
_____
_____
_____
_____

Dear God,

Today my heart overflows with ... _____

_____
_____
_____
_____
_____
_____
_____
_____
_____
_____

# July 22

♡ Scripture:_____

_____

_____

_____

_____

_____


Dear God,

Today my heart overflows with ... _____

_____

_____

_____

_____

_____

_____

_____

_____

_____

_____

# July 23

♡ Scripture:_____
_____

_____
_____
_____
_____

Dear God,

Today my heart overflows with ... _____
_____
_____
_____
_____
_____
_____
_____
_____
_____

# July 24

♡ Scripture: _____

_____

_____

_____

_____

_____


Dear God,

Today my heart overflows with ... _____

_____

_____

_____

_____

_____

_____

_____

_____

_____

# July 25

♡ Scripture: _____

_____

_____

_____

_____

_____


Dear God,

Today my heart overflows with ... _____

_____

_____

_____

_____

_____

_____

_____

_____

_____

# July 26

♡ Scripture:_____

_____

_____

_____

_____

_____


Dear God,

Today my heart overflows with ... _____

_____

_____

_____

_____

_____

_____

_____

_____

_____

_____

# July 27

♡ Scripture: _____

_____

_____

_____

_____

_____


Dear God,

Today my heart overflows with ... _____

_____

_____

_____

_____

_____

_____

_____

_____

_____

_____

# July 28

♡ Scripture: _____

_____

_____

_____

_____

_____

Dear God,

Today my heart overflows with ... _____

_____

_____

_____

_____

_____

_____

_____

_____

_____

_____

# July 29

♡ Scripture: _____
_____

_____
_____
_____
_____

Dear God,

Today my heart overflows with ... _____

_____
_____
_____
_____
_____
_____
_____
_____
_____

# July 30

♡ Scripture:_____
_____
_____
_____
_____
_____


Dear God,

Today my heart overflows with ... _____
_____
_____
_____
_____
_____
_____
_____
_____
_____
_____

# July 31

♡ *Scripture:* _____

_____

_____

_____

_____

_____


*Dear God,*

*Today my heart overflows with ...* _____

_____

_____

_____

_____

_____

_____

_____

_____

_____

_____

Teach me your way, O Lord, and I will walk in your truth; give me an undivided *HEART*, that I may fear your name.
Psalm 86:11 (emphasis added)

Without looking back at your previous divided *heart*, take the time to divide up this *heart* into sections based on where you're presently spending most of your emotional time. Where does your *heart* spend a majority of its time? Is God central in your *heart*, or is He a small piece? Does your *heart* overflow with love, joy, peace, patience, kindness, goodness, faithfulness, gentleness, and self-control? Does your *heart* overflow with hurt, pain, loneliness, brokenness, anger, and despair? Divide the *heart* so that the sections are proportionate to the majority of emotions you are presently experiencing. After dividing up the *heart* on this page, go back and see how it differs from previous *hearts*. Are you developing a *heart* after God's own *heart*?

# *Heart* Monitor #8

## *Selah*

### *Pause, Meditate, Listen*

# August 1

♡ Scripture:_____
_____
_____
_____
_____
_____

Dear God,

Today my heart overflows with ..._____
_____
_____
_____
_____
_____
_____
_____
_____
_____

# August 2

♡ Scripture: _____

_____

_____

_____

_____

_____


Dear God,

Today my heart overflows with ... _____

_____

_____

_____

_____

_____

_____

_____

_____

_____

_____

_____

# August 3

♡ Scripture: _____

_____

_____

_____

_____

_____

Dear God,

Today my heart overflows with ... _____

_____

_____

_____

_____

_____

_____

_____

_____

_____

_____

# August 4

♡ Scripture:_____

_____

_____

_____

_____

_____


Dear God,

Today my heart overflows with ... _____

_____

_____

_____

_____

_____

_____

_____

_____

_____

# August 5

♡ Scripture:_____

_____

_____

_____

_____

_____


Dear God,

Today my heart overflows with ... _____

_____

_____

_____

_____

_____

_____

_____

_____

_____

# August 6

♡ Scripture:_____

_____

_____

_____

_____

_____

Dear God,

Today my heart overflows with ... _____

_____

_____

_____

_____

_____

_____

_____

_____

_____

_____

# August 7

♡ Scripture: _____

_____

_____

_____

_____

_____


Dear God,

Today my heart overflows with ... _____

_____

_____

_____

_____

_____

_____

_____

_____

_____

_____

# August 8

♡ Scripture: _____

_____

_____

_____

_____

_____


Dear God,

Today my heart overflows with ... _____

_____

_____

_____

_____

_____

_____

_____

_____

_____

# August 9

♡ Scripture: _____

_____

_____

_____

_____


Dear God,

Today my heart overflows with ... _____

_____

_____

_____

_____

_____

_____

_____

_____

# August 10

♡ Scripture: _____

_____

_____

_____

_____

_____


Dear God,

Today my heart overflows with ... _____

_____

_____

_____

_____

_____

_____

_____

_____

_____

_____

# August 11

♡ Scripture: _____
_____

_____
_____
_____
_____

Dear God,

Today my heart overflows with ... _____

_____
_____
_____
_____
_____
_____
_____
_____
_____

# August 12

♡ Scripture:_____

_____

_____

_____

_____

_____

Dear God,

Today my heart overflows with ... _____

_____

_____

_____

_____

_____

_____

_____

_____

_____

# August 13

♡ Scripture: _____

_____

_____

_____

_____

_____


Dear God,

Today my heart overflows with ... _____

_____

_____

_____

_____

_____

_____

_____

_____

_____

_____

# August 14

♡ Scripture: _____

_____

_____

_____

_____


Dear God,

Today my heart overflows with ... _____

_____

_____

_____

_____

_____

_____

_____

_____

_____

# August 15

Scripture: _____

_____

_____

_____

_____

_____


Dear God,

Today my heart overflows with ... _____

_____

_____

_____

_____

_____

_____

_____

_____

_____

_____

# August 16

♡ Scripture: _____

_____

_____

_____

_____

_____


Dear God,

Today my heart overflows with ... _____

_____

_____

_____

_____

_____

_____

_____

_____

_____

# August 17

♡ *Scripture:* _____

_____

_____

_____

_____

_____

*Dear God,*

*Today my heart overflows with ...* _____

_____

_____

_____

_____

_____

_____

_____

_____

_____

# August 18

♡ Scripture:_____

_____

_____

_____

_____

_____


Dear God,

Today my heart overflows with ... _____

_____

_____

_____

_____

_____

_____

_____

_____

_____

_ust 19_

♡ _Scripture:_ _____

_____

_____

_____

_____

_____

_Dear God,_

_Today my heart overflows with ..._ _____

_____

_____

_____

_____

_____

_____

_____

_____

_____

_____

# August 20

♡ Scripture: _____

_____

_____

_____

_____

_____


Dear God,

Today my heart overflows with ... _____

_____

_____

_____

_____

_____

_____

_____

_____

_____

_____

st 21

♡ Scripture:_____

_____

_____

_____

_____

_____

Dear God,

Today my heart overflows with ... _____

_____

_____

_____

_____

_____

_____

_____

_____

_____

# August 22

♡ Scripture: _____

_____

_____

_____

_____

_____


Dear God,

Today my heart overflows with ... _____

_____

_____

_____

_____

_____

_____

_____

_____

_____

23

♡ *Scripture:*_____

_____

_____

_____

_____

_____

*Dear God,*

*Today my heart overflows with ...* _____

_____

_____

_____

_____

_____

_____

_____

_____

_____

# August 24

♡ Scripture: _____

_____

_____

_____

_____

_____


Dear God,

Today my heart overflows with ... _____

_____

_____

_____

_____

_____

_____

_____

_____

_____

# August 25

♡ Scripture: _____

_____

_____

_____

_____

_____


Dear God,

Today my heart overflows with ... _____

_____

_____

_____

_____

_____

_____

_____

_____

_____

# August 26

♡ Scripture: _____

_____

_____

_____

_____


Dear God,

Today my heart overflows with ... _____

_____

_____

_____

_____

_____

_____

_____

_____

_____

# August 27

Scripture: _____

_____

_____

_____

_____

_____

Dear God,

Today my heart overflows with ... _____

_____

_____

_____

_____

_____

_____

_____

_____

_____

# August 28

♡ Scripture: _____

_____

_____

_____

_____

_____


Dear God,

Today my heart overflows with ... _____

_____

_____

_____

_____

_____

_____

_____

_____

_____

_____

# August 29

♡ Scripture:_____

_____

_____

_____

_____

_____


Dear God,

Today my heart overflows with ... _____

_____

_____

_____

_____

_____

_____

_____

_____

_____

_____

# August 30

♡ *Scripture:* _____
_____
_____
_____
_____
_____

*Dear God,*

*Today my heart overflows with ...* _____

_____
_____
_____
_____
_____
_____
_____
_____
_____
_____
_____

# August 31

♡ Scripture: _____

_____

_____

_____

_____

_____

Dear God,

Today my heart overflows with ... _____

_____

_____

_____

_____

_____

_____

_____

_____

_____

_____

Teach me your way, O Lord, and I will walk in your truth; give me an undivided *HEART*, that I may fear your name.

Psalm 86:11 (emphasis added)

Without looking back at your previous divided *heart*, take the time to divide up this *heart* into sections based on where you're presently spending most of your emotional time. Where does your *heart* spend a majority of its time? Is God central in your *heart*, or is He a small piece? Does your *heart* overflow with love, joy, peace, patience, kindness, goodness, faithfulness, gentleness, and self-control? Does your *heart* overflow with hurt, pain, loneliness, brokenness, anger, and despair? Divide the *heart* so that the sections are proportionate to the majority of emotions you are presently experiencing. After dividing up the *heart* on this page, go back and see how it differs from previous *hearts*. Where is the abundance of your *heart*?

# *Heart* Monitor #9

## *Selah*

### *Pause, Meditate, Listen*

# September 1

♡ Scripture: _____

_____

_____

_____

_____

_____


Dear God,

Today my heart overflows with ... _____

_____

_____

_____

_____

_____

_____

_____

_____

_____

# September 2

♡ Scripture: _____

_____

_____

_____

_____

_____

Dear God,

Today my heart overflows with ... _____

_____

_____

_____

_____

_____

_____

_____

_____

_____

# September 3

♡ Scripture: _____

_____

_____

_____

_____

_____


Dear God,

Today my heart overflows with ... _____

_____

_____

_____

_____

_____

_____

_____

_____

_____

# September 4

♡ Scripture: _____

_____

_____

_____

_____

_____

Dear God,

Today my heart overflows with ... _____

_____

_____

_____

_____

_____

_____

_____

_____

_____

# September 5

♡ Scripture:_____
_____

_____
_____
_____
_____

Dear God,

Today my heart overflows with ... _____

_____
_____
_____
_____
_____
_____
_____
_____
_____
_____
_____

# September 6

♡ Scripture: _____

_____

_____

_____

_____

_____


Dear God,

Today my heart overflows with ... _____

_____

_____

_____

_____

_____

_____

_____

_____

_____

_____

# September 7

♡ Scripture: _____

_____

_____

_____

_____

_____

Dear God,

Today my heart overflows with ... _____

_____

_____

_____

_____

_____

_____

_____

_____

# September 8

♡ Scripture: _____

_____

_____

_____

_____

_____

Dear God,

Today my heart overflows with ... _____

_____

_____

_____

_____

_____

_____

_____

_____

_____

# September 9

♡ Scripture: _____

_____

_____

_____

_____

_____


Dear God,

Today my heart overflows with ... _____

_____

_____

_____

_____

_____

_____

_____

_____

_____

_____

# September 10

♡ Scripture: _____

_____

_____

_____

_____

_____


Dear God,

Today my heart overflows with ... _____

_____

_____

_____

_____

_____

_____

_____

_____

_____

# September 11

♡ Scripture: _____

_____

_____

_____

_____


Dear God,

Today my heart overflows with ... _____

_____

_____

_____

_____

_____

_____

_____

_____

_____

# September 12

♡ Scripture: _____

_____

_____

_____

_____

_____


Dear God,

Today my heart overflows with ... _____

_____

_____

_____

_____

_____

_____

_____

_____

_____

_____

_____

# September 13

♡ Scripture: _____

_____

_____

_____

_____

_____

Dear God,

Today my heart overflows with ... _____

_____

_____

_____

_____

_____

_____

_____

_____

_____

# September 14

♡ Scripture: _____

_____

_____

_____

_____

_____


Dear God,

Today my heart overflows with ... _____

_____

_____

_____

_____

_____

_____

_____

_____

_____

# September 15

♡ Scripture: _____
_____

_____
_____
_____
_____

Dear God,

Today my heart overflows with ... _____

_____
_____
_____
_____
_____
_____
_____
_____
_____
_____

# September 16

♡ Scripture:_____
_____
_____
_____
_____
_____

Dear God,

Today my heart overflows with ... _____
_____
_____
_____
_____
_____
_____
_____
_____
_____
_____

# September 17

♡ *Scripture:* _____

_____

_____

_____

_____

_____


*Dear God,*

*Today my heart overflows with ...* _____

_____

_____

_____

_____

_____

_____

_____

_____

_____

_____

# September 18

♡ Scripture: _____

_____

_____

_____

_____

_____

Dear God,

Today my heart overflows with ... _____

_____

_____

_____

_____

_____

_____

_____

_____

_____

_____

# September 19

♡ Scripture: _____

_____

_____

_____

_____

_____


Dear God,

Today my heart overflows with ... _____

_____

_____

_____

_____

_____

_____

_____

_____

_____

_____

# September 20

♡ Scripture:_____

_____

_____

_____

_____

_____


Dear God,

Today my heart overflows with ... _____

_____

_____

_____

_____

_____

_____

_____

_____

_____

# September 21

♡ Scripture: _____

_____

_____

_____

_____

_____

Dear God,

Today my heart overflows with ... _____

_____

_____

_____

_____

_____

_____

_____

_____

_____

# September 22

♡ Scripture:_____
_____

_____
_____
_____
_____

Dear God,

Today my heart overflows with ... _____

_____
_____
_____
_____
_____
_____
_____
_____
_____

# September 23

♡ Scripture: _____

_____

_____

_____

_____

_____


Dear God,

Today my heart overflows with ... _____

_____

_____

_____

_____

_____

_____

_____

_____

_____

_____

# September 24

♡ Scripture:_____

_____

_____

_____

_____

_____

Dear God,

Today my heart overflows with ... _____

_____

_____

_____

_____

_____

_____

_____

_____

_____

# September 25

♡ *Scripture:* _____

_____

_____

_____

_____

_____


*Dear God,*

*Today my heart overflows with ...* _____

_____

_____

_____

_____

_____

_____

_____

_____

_____

_____

# September 26

♡ Scripture: _____

_____

_____

_____

_____

_____


Dear God,

Today my heart overflows with ... _____

_____

_____

_____

_____

_____

_____

_____

_____

_____

# September 27

♡ Scripture: _____

_____

_____

_____

_____

_____

Dear God,

Today my heart overflows with ... _____

_____

_____

_____

_____

_____

_____

_____

_____

_____

# September 28

♡ Scripture: _____

_____

_____

_____

_____

_____

Dear God,

Today my heart overflows with ... _____

_____

_____

_____

_____

_____

_____

_____

_____

_____

# September 29

♡ Scripture: _____
_____
_____
_____
_____
_____

Dear God,

Today my heart overflows with ... _____
_____
_____
_____
_____
_____
_____
_____
_____
_____
_____

# September 30

♡ Scripture: _____

_____

_____

_____

_____

_____


Dear God,

Today my heart overflows with ... _____

_____

_____

_____

_____

_____

_____

_____

_____

_____

_____

Teach me your way, O Lord, and I will walk in your truth; give me an undivided *HEART*, that I may fear your name.
Psalm 86:11 (emphasis added)

Without looking back at your previous divided *heart*, take the time to divide up this *heart* into sections based on where you're presently spending most of your emotional time. Where does your *heart* spend a majority of its time? Is God central in your *heart*, or is He a small piece? Does your *heart* overflow with love, joy, peace, patience, kindness, goodness, faithfulness, gentleness, and self-control? Does your *heart* overflow with hurt, pain, loneliness, brokenness, anger, and despair? Divide the *heart* so that the sections are proportionate to the majority of emotions you are presently experiencing. After dividing up the *heart* on this page, go back and see how it differs from previous *hearts*. What is presently overflowing from your *heart*?

# *Heart* Monitor #10

*Selah*

*Pause, Meditate, Listen*

# October 1

♡ Scripture:_____
_____

_____
_____
_____
_____

Dear God,

Today my heart overflows with ... _____
_____
_____
_____
_____
_____
_____
_____
_____
_____
_____

# October 2

♡ Scripture: _____

_____

_____

_____

_____

_____


Dear God,

Today my heart overflows with ... _____

_____

_____

_____

_____

_____

_____

_____

_____

_____

# October 3

♡ Scripture: _____

_____

_____

_____

_____

_____

Dear God,

Today my heart overflows with ... _____

_____

_____

_____

_____

_____

_____

_____

_____

_____

_____

# October 4

♡ Scripture:_____

_____

_____

_____

_____

_____


Dear God,

Today my heart overflows with ... _____

_____

_____

_____

_____

_____

_____

_____

_____

_____

_____

# October 5

♡ Scripture: _____

_____

_____

_____

_____

_____


Dear God,

Today my heart overflows with ... _____

_____

_____

_____

_____

_____

_____

_____

_____

_____

_____

# October 6

♡ Scripture: _____

_____

_____

_____

_____

_____


Dear God,

Today my heart overflows with ... _____

_____

_____

_____

_____

_____

_____

_____

_____

_____

# October 7

♡ Scripture:_____

_____

_____

_____

_____

_____


Dear God,

Today my heart overflows with ... _____

_____

_____

_____

_____

_____

_____

_____

_____

_____

_____

# October 8

♡ *Scripture:* _____

_____

_____

_____

_____

_____

*Dear God,*

*Today my heart overflows with ...* _____

_____

_____

_____

_____

_____

_____

_____

_____

_____

_____

# October 9

♡ Scripture: _____

_____

_____

_____

_____



Dear God,

Today my heart overflows with ... _____

_____

_____

_____

_____

_____

_____

_____

_____

_____

# October 10

♡ *Scripture:* _____

_____

_____

_____

_____

_____


*Dear God,*

*Today my heart overflows with ...* _____

_____

_____

_____

_____

_____

_____

_____

_____

_____

# October 11

♡ Scripture: _____

_____

_____

_____

_____

_____

Dear God,

Today my heart overflows with ... _____

_____

_____

_____

_____

_____

_____

_____

_____

_____

_____

# October 12

♡ Scripture: _____

_____

_____

_____

_____

_____


Dear God,

Today my heart overflows with ... _____

_____

_____

_____

_____

_____

_____

_____

_____

_____

_____

# October 13

♡ Scripture:_____

_____

_____

_____

_____

_____


Dear God,

Today my heart overflows with ... _____

_____

_____

_____

_____

_____

_____

_____

_____

_____

# October 14

♡ *Scripture:* _____

_____

_____

_____

_____


*Dear God,*

*Today my heart overflows with ...* _____

_____

_____

_____

_____

_____

_____

_____

_____

_____

# October 15

♡ Scripture: _____

_____

_____

_____

_____

Dear God,

Today my heart overflows with ... _____

_____

_____

_____

_____

_____

_____

_____

_____

_____

# October 16

♡ Scripture: _____

_____

_____

_____

_____

_____


Dear God,

Today my heart overflows with ... _____

_____

_____

_____

_____

_____

_____

_____

_____

_____

# October 17

♡ Scripture: _____

_____

_____

_____

_____

_____

Dear God,

Today my heart overflows with ... _____

_____

_____

_____

_____

_____

_____

_____

_____

# October 18

♡ Scripture: _____

_____

_____

_____

_____

_____


Dear God,

Today my heart overflows with ... _____

_____

_____

_____

_____

_____

_____

_____

_____

_____

# October 19

♡ Scripture: _____

_____

_____

_____

_____

_____


Dear God,

Today my heart overflows with ... _____

_____

_____

_____

_____

_____

_____

_____

_____

_____

_____

# October 20

♡ Scripture: _____

_____

_____

_____

_____

_____


Dear God,

Today my heart overflows with ... _____

_____

_____

_____

_____

_____

_____

_____

_____

_____

_____

# October 21

♡ Scripture: _____
_____
_____
_____
_____
_____

Dear God,

Today my heart overflows with ... _____
_____
_____
_____
_____
_____
_____
_____
_____
_____
_____
_____

# October 22

♡ Scripture: _____

_____

_____

_____

_____

_____

Dear God,

Today my heart overflows with ... _____

_____

_____

_____

_____

_____

_____

_____

_____

_____

# October 23

♡ Scripture: _____

_____

_____

_____

_____

_____

Dear God,

Today my heart overflows with ... _____

_____

_____

_____

_____

_____

_____

_____

_____

_____

# October 24

♡ Scripture: _____

_____

_____

_____

_____

_____

Dear God,

Today my heart overflows with ... _____

_____

_____

_____

_____

_____

_____

_____

_____

# October 25

♡ Scripture:_____

_____

_____

_____

_____

_____


Dear God,

Today my heart overflows with ... _____

_____

_____

_____

_____

_____

_____

_____

_____

_____

_____

# October 26

♡ *Scripture:* _____

_____

_____

_____

_____

_____

*Dear God,*

*Today my heart overflows with ...* _____

_____

_____

_____

_____

_____

_____

_____

_____

_____

# October 27

♡ Scripture: _____

_____

_____

_____

_____

_____


Dear God,

Today my heart overflows with ... _____

_____

_____

_____

_____

_____

_____

_____

_____

_____

# October 28

♡ Scripture: _____

_____

_____

_____

_____

_____

Dear God,

Today my heart overflows with ... _____

_____

_____

_____

_____

_____

_____

_____

_____

_____

# October 29

♡ Scripture: _____

_____

_____

_____

_____

_____

Dear God,

Today my heart overflows with ... _____

_____

_____

_____

_____

_____

_____

_____

_____

_____

_____

# October 30

♡ Scripture: _____

_____

_____

_____

_____

_____


Dear God,

Today my heart overflows with ... _____

_____

_____

_____

_____

_____

_____

_____

_____

_____

_____

# October 31

♡ Scripture: _____

_____

_____

_____

_____

_____

Dear God,

Today my heart overflows with ... _____

_____

_____

_____

_____

_____

_____

_____

_____

_____

_____

_____

Teach me your way, O Lord, and I will walk in your truth; give me an undivided *HEART*, that I may fear your name.

Psalm 86:11 (emphasis added)

Without looking back at your previous divided *heart*, take the time to divide up this *heart* into sections based on where you're presently spending most of your emotional time. Where does your *heart* spend a majority of its time? Is God central in your *heart*, or is He a small piece? Does your *heart* overflow with love, joy, peace, patience, kindness, goodness, faithfulness, gentleness, and self-control? Does your *heart* overflow with hurt, pain, loneliness, brokenness, anger, and despair? Divide the *heart* so that the sections are proportionate to the majority of emotions you are presently experiencing. After dividing up the *heart* on this page, go back and see how it differs from previous *hearts*. Are you developing a *heart* after God's own *heart*?

# *Heart* Monitor #11

## Selah

### Pause, Meditate, Listen

# November 1

♡ Scripture: _____

_____

_____

_____

_____

_____


Dear God,

Today my heart overflows with ... _____

_____

_____

_____

_____

_____

_____

_____

_____

_____

_____

_____

# November 2

♡ Scripture: _____

_____

_____

_____

_____

_____

Dear God,

Today my heart overflows with ... _____

_____

_____

_____

_____

_____

_____

_____

_____

_____

_____

# November 3

♡ *Scripture:* _____

_____

_____

_____

_____

_____


*Dear God,*

*Today my heart overflows with ...* _____

_____

_____

_____

_____

_____

_____

_____

_____

_____

_____

# November 4

♡ Scripture: _____

_____

_____

_____

_____

_____


Dear God,

Today my heart overflows with ... _____

_____

_____

_____

_____

_____

_____

_____

_____

_____

_____

# November 5

♡ Scripture: _____

_____

_____

_____

_____

_____


Dear God,

Today my heart overflows with ... _____

_____

_____

_____

_____

_____

_____

_____

_____

_____

# November 6

♡ *Scripture:* _____

_____

_____

_____

_____

_____


*Dear God,*

*Today my heart overflows with ...* _____

_____

_____

_____

_____

_____

_____

_____

_____

_____

_____

# November 7

♡ Scripture: _____

_____

_____

_____

_____

_____


Dear God,

Today my heart overflows with ... _____

_____

_____

_____

_____

_____

_____

_____

_____

_____

_____

# November 8

♡ Scripture:_____

_____

_____
_____
_____
_____

Dear God,

Today my heart overflows with ... _____

_____
_____
_____
_____
_____
_____
_____
_____
_____
_____

# November 9

♡ Scripture:_____

_____

_____

_____

_____

_____

Dear God,

Today my heart overflows with ... _____

_____

_____

_____

_____

_____

_____

_____

_____

_____

# November 10

♡ *Scripture:* _____

_____

_____

_____

_____

_____


*Dear God,*

*Today my heart overflows with ...* _____

_____

_____

_____

_____

_____

_____

_____

_____

_____

# November 11

♡ Scripture: _____

_____

_____

_____

_____

_____


Dear God,

Today my heart overflows with ... _____

_____

_____

_____

_____

_____

_____

_____

_____

_____

_____

# November 12

♡ Scripture: _____

_____

_____

_____

_____

_____


Dear God,

Today my heart overflows with ... _____

_____

_____

_____

_____

_____

_____

_____

_____

_____

# November 13

♡ Scripture: _____

_____

_____

_____

_____

_____


Dear God,

Today my heart overflows with ... _____

_____

_____

_____

_____

_____

_____

_____

_____

_____

# November 14

♡ Scripture: _____

_____

_____

_____

_____

_____


Dear God,

Today my heart overflows with ... _____

_____

_____

_____

_____

_____

_____

_____

_____

_____

# November 15

♡ Scripture: _____

_____

_____

_____

_____

_____

Dear God,

Today my heart overflows with ... _____

_____

_____

_____

_____

_____

_____

_____

_____

_____

# November 16

♡ Scripture: _____

_____

_____

_____

_____

_____


Dear God,

Today my heart overflows with ... _____

_____

_____

_____

_____

_____

_____

_____

_____

_____

_____

# November 17

♡ Scripture: _____

_____

_____

_____

_____

_____


Dear God,

Today my heart overflows with ... _____

_____

_____

_____

_____

_____

_____

_____

_____

_____

_____

# November 18

♡ Scripture: _____

_____

_____

_____

_____

_____


Dear God,

Today my heart overflows with ... _____

_____

_____

_____

_____

_____

_____

_____

_____

_____

_____

# November 19

♡ *Scripture:* _____

_____

_____

_____

_____

_____

*Dear God,*

*Today my heart overflows with ...* _____

_____

_____

_____

_____

_____

_____

_____

_____

_____

# November 20

♡ Scripture: _____

_____

_____

_____

_____

_____


Dear God,

Today my heart overflows with ... _____

_____

_____

_____

_____

_____

_____

_____

_____

_____

_____

# November 21

♡ Scripture: _____

_____

_____

_____

_____

_____

Dear God,

Today my heart overflows with ... _____

_____

_____

_____

_____

_____

_____

_____

_____

_____

# November 22

♡ Scripture: _____

_____

_____

_____

_____

_____


Dear God,

Today my heart overflows with ... _____

_____

_____

_____

_____

_____

_____

_____

_____

_____

# November 23

♡ Scripture: _____

_____

_____

_____

_____

_____


Dear God,

Today my heart overflows with ... _____

_____

_____

_____

_____

_____

_____

_____

_____

_____

_____

# November 24

♡ Scripture: _____

_____

_____

_____

_____

_____


Dear God,

Today my heart overflows with ... _____

_____

_____

_____

_____

_____

_____

_____

_____

_____

_____

# November 25

♡ Scripture:_____

_____

_____

_____

_____

_____


Dear God,

Today my heart overflows with ... _____

_____

_____

_____

_____

_____

_____

_____

_____

_____

_____

# November 26

♡ Scripture: _____

_____

_____

_____

_____

_____


Dear God,

Today my heart overflows with ... _____

_____

_____

_____

_____

_____

_____

_____

_____

_____

# November 27

♡ *Scripture:* _____

_____

_____

_____

_____

_____

*Dear God,*

*Today my heart overflows with ...* _____

_____

_____

_____

_____

_____

_____

_____

_____

_____

# November 28

♡ Scripture: _____

_____

_____

_____

_____

_____


Dear God,

Today my heart overflows with ... _____

_____

_____

_____

_____

_____

_____

_____

_____

_____

# November 29

♡ Scripture:_____
_____

_____
_____
_____
_____

Dear God,

Today my heart overflows with ... _____

_____
_____
_____
_____
_____
_____
_____
_____
_____
_____

# November 30

♡ Scripture:_____

_____

_____

_____

_____

_____

Dear God,

Today my heart overflows with ... _____

_____

_____

_____

_____

_____

_____

_____

_____

_____

Teach me your way, O Lord, and I will walk in your truth; give me an undivided 𝓗𝓔𝓐𝓡𝓣, that I may fear your name.

Psalm 86:11 (emphasis added)

Without looking back at your previous divided *heart*, take the time to divide up this *heart* into sections based on where you're presently spending most of your emotional time. Where does your *heart* spend a majority of its time? Is God central in your *heart*, or is He a small piece? Does your *heart* overflow with love, joy, peace, patience, kindness, goodness, faithfulness, gentleness, and self-control? Does your *heart* overflow with hurt, pain, loneliness, brokenness, anger, and despair? Divide the *heart* so that the sections are proportionate to the majority of emotions you are presently experiencing. After dividing up the *heart* on this page, go back and see how it differs from previous *hearts*. Have you experienced a major *heart* change?

# 𝓗eart Monitor #12

## 𝒮elah

### 𝒫ause, 𝑀editate, 𝓛isten

# December 1

♡ Scripture: _____

_____

_____

_____

_____

_____



Dear God,

Today my heart overflows with ... _____

_____

_____

_____

_____

_____

_____

_____

_____

_____

# December 2

♡ Scripture: _____

_____

_____

_____

_____

_____


Dear God,

Today my heart overflows with ... _____

_____

_____

_____

_____

_____

_____

_____

_____

_____

# December 3

♡ Scripture: _____

_____

_____

_____

_____

_____


Dear God,

Today my heart overflows with ... _____

_____

_____

_____

_____

_____

_____

_____

_____

_____

_____

# December 4

♡ Scripture:_____

_____

_____

_____

_____

_____


Dear God,

Today my heart overflows with ... _____

_____

_____

_____

_____

_____

_____

_____

_____

_____

_____

# December 5

♡ Scripture: _____
_____

_____
_____
_____
_____

Dear God,

Today my heart overflows with ... _____

_____
_____
_____
_____
_____
_____
_____
_____
_____
_____

# December 6

♡ Scripture: _____

_____

_____

_____

_____


Dear God,

Today my heart overflows with ... _____

_____

_____

_____

_____

_____

_____

_____

_____

_____

# December 7

♡ Scripture: _____

_____

_____

_____

_____

_____


Dear God,

Today my heart overflows with ... _____

_____

_____

_____

_____

_____

_____

_____

_____

_____

_____

# December 8

♡ Scripture: _____

_____

_____

_____

_____

_____


Dear God,

Today my heart overflows with ... _____

_____

_____

_____

_____

_____

_____

_____

_____

_____

_____

# December 9

♡ Scripture: _____

_____

_____

_____

_____

_____


Dear God,

Today my heart overflows with ... _____

_____

_____

_____

_____

_____

_____

_____

_____

_____

_____

# December 10

♡ Scripture:_____

_____

_____

_____

_____

_____


Dear God,

Today my heart overflows with ... _____

_____

_____

_____

_____

_____

_____

_____

_____

_____

_____

# December 11

♡ Scripture: _____
_____
_____
_____
_____
_____

Dear God,

Today my heart overflows with ... _____
_____
_____
_____
_____
_____
_____
_____
_____
_____
_____
_____

# December 12

♡ Scripture: _____

_____

_____

_____

_____

_____


Dear God,

Today my heart overflows with ... _____

_____

_____

_____

_____

_____

_____

_____

_____

_____

_____

# December 13

♡ *Scripture:* _____

_____

_____

_____

_____

_____

*Dear God,*

*Today my heart overflows with ...* _____

_____

_____

_____

_____

_____

_____

_____

_____

_____

# December 14

♡ Scripture:_____

_____

_____

_____

_____

_____

Dear God,

Today my heart overflows with ... _____

_____

_____

_____

_____

_____

_____

_____

_____

_____

_____

# December 15

♡ Scripture: _____

_____

_____

_____

_____

_____


Dear God,

Today my heart overflows with ... _____

_____

_____

_____

_____

_____

_____

_____

_____

_____

_____

# December 16

♡ Scripture:_____

_____

_____

_____

_____

_____


Dear God,

Today my heart overflows with ... _____

_____

_____

_____

_____

_____

_____

_____

_____

_____

_____

# December 17

♡ Scripture: _____

_____

_____

_____

_____

_____


Dear God,

Today my heart overflows with ... _____

_____

_____

_____

_____

_____

_____

_____

_____

_____

# December 18

♡ Scripture: _____

_____

_____

_____

_____

_____


Dear God,

Today my heart overflows with ... _____

_____

_____

_____

_____

_____

_____

_____

_____

_____

# December 19

♡ Scripture: _____

_____

_____

_____

_____

_____


Dear God,

Today my heart overflows with ... _____

_____

_____

_____

_____

_____

_____

_____

_____

_____

# December 20

♡ Scripture: _____

_____

_____

_____

_____

_____


Dear God,

Today my heart overflows with ... _____

_____

_____

_____

_____

_____

_____

_____

_____

# December 21

♡ Scripture: _____

_____

_____

_____

_____

_____


Dear God,

Today my heart overflows with ... _____

_____

_____

_____

_____

_____

_____

_____

_____

_____

_____

# December 22

♡ Scripture:_____

_____

_____

_____

_____

_____


Dear God,

Today my heart overflows with ... _____

_____

_____

_____

_____

_____

_____

_____

_____

_____

_____

# December 23

♡ Scripture:_____

_____

_____

_____

_____


Dear God,

Today my heart overflows with ... _____

_____

_____

_____

_____

_____

_____

_____

_____

_____

# December 24

♡ Scripture: _____

_____

_____

_____

_____

_____


Dear God,

Today my heart overflows with ... _____

_____

_____

_____

_____

_____

_____

_____

_____

_____

_____

# December 25

♡ Scripture: _____

_____

_____

_____

_____

_____


Dear God,

Today my heart overflows with ... _____

_____

_____

_____

_____

_____

_____

_____

_____

_____

_____

# December 26

♡ Scripture: _____

_____

_____

_____

_____

_____


Dear God,

Today my heart overflows with ... _____

_____

_____

_____

_____

_____

_____

_____

_____

_____

_____

# December 27

♡ Scripture: _____

_____

_____

_____

_____

_____

Dear God,

Today my heart overflows with ... _____

_____

_____

_____

_____

_____

_____

_____

_____

_____

_____

# December 28

♡ *Scripture:* _____

_____

_____

_____

_____

_____


*Dear God,*

*Today my heart overflows with ...* _____

_____

_____

_____

_____

_____

_____

_____

_____

_____

# December 29

♡ Scripture:_____

_____

_____

_____

_____

_____


Dear God,

Today my heart overflows with ... _____

_____

_____

_____

_____

_____

_____

_____

_____

_____

_____

# December 30

♡ Scripture:_____
_____
_____
_____
_____

Dear God,

Today my heart overflows with ... _____
_____
_____
_____
_____
_____
_____
_____
_____
_____

# December 31

♡ Scripture: _____

_____

_____

_____

_____

_____


Dear God,

Today my heart overflows with ... _____

_____

_____

_____

_____

_____

_____

_____

_____

_____

Teach me your way, O Lord, and I will walk in your truth; give me an undivided *HEART*, that I may fear your name.

Psalm 86:11 (emphasis added)

Without looking back at your previous divided *heart*, take the time to divide up this *heart* into sections based on where you're presently spending most of your emotional time. Where does your *heart* spend a majority of its time? Is God central in your *heart*, or is He a small piece? Does your *heart* overflow with love, joy, peace, patience, kindness, goodness, faithfulness, gentleness, and self-control? Does your *heart* overflow with hurt, pain, loneliness, brokenness, anger, and despair? Divide the *heart* so that the sections are proportionate to the majority of emotions you are presently experiencing. After dividing up the *heart* on this page, go back and see how it differs from previous *hearts*. Have you developed a *heart* that overflows with God's goodness?

# *Heart* Monitor #13

## *Selah*

### *Pause, Meditate, Listen*

# Scripture Verses on the *Heart*

Unless otherwise noted, all verses come from the NIV. I have emphasized "heart" throughout.

**Exodus 25:2**
You are to receive the offering for me from each man whose *HEART* prompts him to give.

**Leviticus 19:17**
Do not hate your brother in your *HEART*. Rebuke your neighbor frankly so you will not share in his guilt.

**Deuteronomy 4:29**
But if from there you seek the Lord your God, you will find him if you look for him with all your *HEART* and with all your soul.

**Deuteronomy 6:5**
Love the Lord your God with all your *HEART* and with all your soul and with all your strength.

**Deuteronomy 10:12**
What does the Lord your God ask of you but to fear the Lord your God, to walk in his ways, to love him, to serve the Lord your God with all your *HEART* and with all your soul, and to observe the Lord's commands and decrees that I am giving you today for your own good?

**Deuteronomy 11:18**
Fix these words of mind in your *HEARTS* and minds; tie them as symbols on your hands and bind them on your foreheads.

**Deuteronomy 15:10**
Give generously to him and do so without a grudging *HEART*; then because of this the Lord your God will bless you in all your work and in everything you put your hand to.

**Deuteronomy 30:6**
The Lord your God will circumcise your *HEARTS* and the *HEARTS*

of your descendants, so that you may love him with all your HEART and with all your soul, and live.

♡ Deuteronomy 30:9b–10
The Lord will again delight in you and make you prosperous, just as he delighted in your fathers, if you obey the Lord your God and keep his commands and decrees that are written in this Book of the Law and turn to the Lord your God with all your HEART and with all your soul.

♡ Joshua 22:5
But be very careful to keep the commandment and the law that Moses the servant of the LORD gave you: to love the Lord your God, to walk in all his ways, to obey his commands, to hold fast to him and to serve him with all your HEART and all your soul.

♡ 1 Samuel 13:14
But now your kingdom will not endure; the Lord has sought out a man after his own HEART and appointed him leader of his people, because you have not kept the Lord's command.

♡ 1 Samuel 16:7b
The Lord does not look at the things man looks at. Man looks at the outward appearance, but the Lord looks at the HEART.

♡ 1 Kings 8:39
Forgive and act; deal with each man according to all he does, since you know his HEART (for you alone know the HEARTS of all men).

♡ 1 Kings 8:61
But your HEARTS must be fully committed to the Lord our God, to live by his decrees and obey his commands, as at this time.

♡ 2 Kings 23:3
The king stood by the pillar and renewed the covenant in the presence of the Lord—to follow the Lord and keep his commands, regulations and decrees with all his HEART and all his soul, thus confirming the words of the covenant written in this book.

♡ 1 Chronicles 28:9
Acknowledge the God of your father, and serve him with wholehearted

devotion and with a willing mind, for the Lord searches every *HEART* and understands every motive behind the thoughts.

Pellet 2 Chronicles 7:16
I have chosen and consecrated this temple so that my Name may be there forever. My eyes and my *HEART* will always be there.

Job 22:22
Accept instruction from his mouth and lay up his words in your *HEART*.

Job 37:1
At this my *HEART* pounds and leaps from its place.

Psalm 14:1
The fool says in his *HEART*, "There is no God." They are corrupt, their deeds are vile; there is no one who does good.

Psalm 19:14
May the words of my mouth and the meditation of my *HEART* be pleasing in your sight, O Lord, my Rock and my Redeemer.

Psalm 37:4
Delight yourself in the Lord and he will give you the desires of your *HEART*.

Psalm 45:1
My *HEART* is stirred by a noble theme as I recite my verses for the king; my tongue is the pen of a skillful writer.

Psalm 51:10
Create in me a pure *HEART*, O God, and renew a steadfast spirit within me.

Psalm 51:17
The sacrifices of God are a broken spirit; a broken and contrite *HEART*, O God, you will not despise.

Psalm 62:4
They fully intend to topple him from his lofty place; they take delight in lies. With their mouths they bless but in their *HEARTS* they curse. *Selah*

♡ Psalm 62:8

Trust in him at all times, O people; pour out your HEARTS to him, for God is our refuge. Selah.

♡ Psalm 64:10

Let the righteous rejoice in the Lord and take refuge in him; let all the upright in HEART praise him!

♡ Psalm 66:18–19

If I had cherished sin in my HEART, the Lord would not have listened; but God has surely listened and heard my voice in prayer.

♡ Psalm 86:11

Teach me your way, O Lord, and I will walk in your truth; give me an undivided HEART, that I may fear your name.

♡ Psalm 86:12

I will praise you, O Lord my God, with all my HEART; I will glorify your name forever.

♡ Psalm 119:11

I have hidden your word in my HEART that I might not sin against you.

♡ Psalm 119:32

I run in the path of your commands, for you have set my HEART free.

♡ Psalm 138:1

I will praise you, O Lord, with all my HEART; before the "gods" I will sing your praise.

♡ Psalm 139:23

Search me, O God, and know my HEART; test me and know my anxious thoughts.

♡ Proverbs 3:5

Trust in the Lord with all your HEART and lean not to your own understanding; in all your ways acknowledge him, and he will make your paths straight.

Proverbs 4:20–22

My son, pay attention to what I say; listen closely to my words. Do not let them out of your sight, keep them within your HEART; for they are life to those who find them and health to a man's whole body.

Proverbs 4:23

Above all else, guard your HEART, for it is the wellspring of life.

Proverbs 7:2–3

Keep my commands and you will live; guard my teachings as the apple of your eye. Bind them on your fingers; write them on the tablet of your HEART.

Proverbs 13:12

Hope deferred makes the HEART sick, but a longing fulfilled is a tree of life.

Proverbs 14:13

Even in laughter the HEART may ache, and joy may end in grief.

Proverbs 15:30

A cheerful look brings joy to the HEART, and good news gives health to the bones.

Proverbs 17:22

A cheerful HEART is good medicine, but a crushed spirit dries up the bones.

Proverbs 24:17

Do not gloat when your enemy falls; when he stumbles, do not let your HEART rejoice, or the Lord will see and disapprove and turn his wrath away from him.

Proverbs 27:19

As water reflects a face, so a man's HEART reflects the man.

Ecclesiastes 3:11

He has made everything beautiful in its time. He has also set eternity in the HEARTS of men; yet they cannot fathom what God has done from beginning to end.

♡ Ecclesiastes 8:5
Whoever obeys his command will come to no harm, and the wise *HEART* will know the proper time and procedure.

♡ Song of Solomon 4:9
You have stolen my *HEART*, my sister, my bride; you have stolen my *HEART* with one glance of your eyes, with one jewel of your necklace.

♡ Isaiah 40:11
He tends his flock like a shepherd; He gathers the lambs in his arms and carries them close to his *HEART*; he gently leads those that have young.

♡ Isaiah 57:15
For this is what the high and lofty One says—he who lives forever, whose name is holy: "I live in a high and holy place, but also with him who is contrite and lowly in spirit, to revive the spirit of the lowly and to revive the *HEART* of the contrite."

♡ Jeremiah 17:9
The *HEART* is deceitful above all things and beyond cure. Who can understand it?

♡ Jeremiah 29:13
You will seek Matthew 6:21me and find me when you seek me with all your *HEART*.

♡ Jeremiah 31:33
"This is the covenant I will make with the house of Israel after that time, declares the Lord. I will put my law in their minds and write it on their *HEARTS*. I will be their God, and they will be my people."

♡ Ezekiel 36:26–27
I will give you a new *HEART* and put a new spirit in you; I will remove from you your *HEART* of stone and give you a *HEART* of flesh. And I will put my spirit in you and move you to follow my decrees and be careful to keep my laws.

♡ Matthew 5:8
Blessed are the pure in *HEART*, for they will see God.

♡ Matthew 6:21
For where your treasure is, there your *HEART* will be also.

♡ Matthew 12:34
You brood of vipers, how can you who are evil say anything good? For out of the overflow of the *HEART* the mouth speaks.

♡ Matthew 22:37
Jesus replied, "Love the Lord your God with all your *HEART* and with all your soul and with all your mind."

♡ Luke 6:45
The good man brings good things out of the good stored up in his *HEART*, and the evil man brings evil things out of the evil stored up in his *HEART*. For out of the overflow of his *HEART* his mouth speaks.

♡ Luke 16:15
He said to them, "You are the ones who justify yourselves in the eyes of men, but God knows your *HEARTS*. What is highly valued among men is detestable in God's sight.

♡ Luke 24:32
They asked each other, "Were not our *HEARTS* burning within us while he talked with us on the road and opened the Scriptures to us?"

♡ John 14:1
Do not let your *HEARTS* be troubled. Trust in God; trust also in me.

♡ Acts 15:9
He made no distinction between us and them, for he purified their *HEARTS* by faith.

♡ Romans 2:15
Since they show that the requirements of the law are written on their *HEARTS*, their consciences also bearing witness, and their thoughts now accusing, now even defending them.

♡ Romans 2:29
No, a man is a Jew if he is one inwardly; and circumcision is circumcision of the *HEART*, by the Spirit, not by the written code. Such a man's praise is not from men, but from God.

♡ Romans 10:10
For it is with your *HEART* that you believe and are justified, and it is with your mouth that you confess and are saved.

♡ 1 Corinthians 14:25
And the secrets of his *HEART* will be laid bare. So he will fall down and worship God, exclaiming, "God is really among you!"

♡ 2 Corinthians 3:2
You yourselves are our letter, written on our *HEARTS* known and read by everybody.

♡ 2 Corinthians 3:3
You show that you are a letter from Christ, the result of our ministry, written not with ink but with the Spirit of the living God, not on tablets of stone but on tablets of human *HEARTS*.

♡ 2 Corinthians 4:6
For God, who said, "Let light shine out of darkness," made his light shine in our *HEARTS* to give us the light of the knowledge of the glory of God in the face of Christ.

♡ Ephesians 3:16–19
I pray that out of his glorious riches he may strengthen you with power through his spirit in your inner being, so that Christ may dwell in your *HEARTS* through faith. And I pray that you, being rooted and established in love, may have power, together with all the saints, to grasp how wide and long and high and deep is the love of Christ, and to know this love that surpasses knowledge—that you may be filled to the measure of all the fullness of God.

♡ Ephesians 5:19–20
Speak to one another with psalms, hymns and spiritual songs. Sing and make music in your *HEART* to the Lord, always giving thanks to God the Father for everything, in the name of our Lord Jesus Christ.

♡ Ephesians 6:6
Obey them not only to win their favor when their eye is on you, but like slaves of Christ, doing the will of God from your *HEART*.

Colossians 3:1
Since, then, you have been raised with Christ, set your *HEARTS* on things above, where Christ is seated at the right hand of God.

Colossians 3:23
Whatever you do, work at it with all your *HEART*, as working for the Lord, not for men, since you know that you will receive an inheritance from the Lord as a reward.

Hebrews 3:7–9
So, as the Holy Spirit says: "Today, if you hear his voice, do not harden your *HEARTS* as you did in the rebellion, during the time of testing in the desert, where your fathers tested and tried me and for forty years saw what I did."

Hebrews 10:16
"This is the covenant I will make with them after that time, says the Lord. I will put my laws in their *HEARTS*, and I will write them on their minds."

1 Peter 1:22
Now that you have purified yourselves by obeying the truth so that you have sincere love for your brothers, love one another deeply, from the *HEART*.

1 John 3:19–20
This then is how we know that we belong to the truth, and how we set our *HEARTS* at rest in his presence whenever our *HEARTS* condemn us. For God is greater than our *HEARTS*, and he knows everything.

1 John 3: 21
Dear friends, if our *HEARTS* do not condemn us, we have the confidence before God and receive from him anything we ask, because we obey his commands and do what pleases him.

# Scriptural References to the *Heart*

Exodus 25:2

Leviticus 19:17

Deuteronomy 4:29
Deuteronomy 6:5
Deuteronomy 10:12
Deuteronomy 11:18
Deuteronomy 15:10
Deuteronomy 30:6
Deuteronomy 30:9b–10

Joshua 22:5

1 Samuel 13:14
1 Samuel 16:7b

1 Kings 8:39
1 Kings 8:61
2 Kings 23:3

1 Chronicles 28:9
2 Chronicles 7:16

Job 22:22
Job 37:1

Psalm 14:1
Psalm 19:14
Psalm 37:4
Psalm 45:1
Psalm 51:10
Psalm 51:17
Psalm 62:4

Psalm 62:8
Psalm 64:10
Psalm 66:18
Psalm 86:11–12
Psalm 119:11
Psalm 119:32
Psalm 138:1
Psalm 139:23

Proverbs 3:5
Proverbs 4:21
Proverbs 4:23
Proverbs 7:3
Proverbs 13:12
Proverbs 14:13
Proverbs 15:30
Proverbs 17:22
Proverbs 24:17
Proverbs 27:19

Ecclesiastes 3:11
Ecclesiastes 8:5

Song of Solomon 4:9

Isaiah 40:11
Isaiah 57:15

Jeremiah 17:9
Jeremiah 29:13
Jeremiah 31:33

Ezekiel 36:26

Matthew 5:8
Matthew 6:21
Matthew 12:34
Matthew 22:37

Luke 6:45
Luke 16:15
Luke 24:32

John 14:1

Acts 15:9

Romans 2:15
Romans 2:29
Romans 10:10

1 Corinthians 14:25
2 Corinthians 3:2–3

2 Corinthians 4:6

Ephesians 3:17
Ephesians 5:19
Ephesians 6:6

Colossians 3:1
Colossians 3:23

Hebrews 3:8
Hebrews 10:16

1 Peter 1:22

1 John 3:19–20
1 John 3: 21

CPSIA information can be obtained at www.ICGtesting.com
Printed in the USA
LVOW130602081112

306335LV00002B/6/P